JOHANNA
A HISTORICAL ROMANCE NOVEL
by
MARY JO HODGE

BOOK ONE
FROM THE TRILOGY:
JOURNEY THROUGH DARKNESS

PRINTED BY CREATE SPACE, A DIVISION OF AMAZON

This novel was written by and is the sole property of
Mary Jo Hodge
Eden, NY
Copyright #TXu1-361-778
July 27, 2007
Registered under name of 1st version:
HOME OF THE BRAVE

DEDICATED
IN MEMORY OF MY
BELOVED BROTHER
JOHN BOWLING McKINNEY, JR
"OH SO GREAT WAS HIS CAPACITY
FOR LOVE"

JOHANNA

THE BIRTH OF THIS STORY
2014

Dear Merry Reader,

About seven years ago I began writing this novel. I tried several titles, first was "Home of the Brave". Some of the other names included "Cast Your Own Shadow", "Cloak of Destiny," "Wings of Eagles" and "Duty and Deceit". Each title was appropriate in some ways for the version so named and totaled around 80,000 words.

After 'completing' what turned out to be version one, I pulled out all my magazines for writers and read every article about how to interest an agent or editor. I purchased close to a dozen books on how to write queries, how to get published and variations on this theme. I contacted at least a dozen agents/editors. Each query differed, as each was approached according to the preferences noted in the individual web sites. No one wanted me to send the large manuscript. Most did not bother to even acknowledge receipt of the query.

The one consistent advice in most of my how-to articles was to 'read'. Read in your genre. Read in all genres. Read books represented by the agent/editor you are querying. Put your novel on the shelve and let it 'cook' and read, read, read.

I purchased a Kindle and read over two hundred novels in the next year. I read from all genre's except horror, and even a little of that. I read every novel on the ten best sellers list for about three months. I read every novel by a first time writer I could find at the library and on my Kindle.

Reading so many books in a short time frame gave me more insight about how few stories out there are new. The skill of the writer to tell an old and tried story in an interesting and imaginative way is of utmost importance to the novel's attraction to You, the Merry Reader.

From this experience six women emerged in my imagination, each a caricature of multiple popular protagonists used over and over in fiction, dating back at least to "The Pilgrim's Progress" (John Bunyan, 1648). With tongue-in-cheek I put the six ladies together in a novel, "Under Cover: Secrets of the Fox Willow Quilters" and had it printed by Create Space - my first experience with print-on-demand. One woman, when a young girl working with her parents for the French underground in WWII, is being sought by members of a secret group working out of South America. Her friends include a former and most unwilling 'Lady-of-the-Night', a jewel thief, and an undercover FBI agent now in witness protection, who is known for her marvelous jam. An abused woman hiding from her tormenter joins this unlikely foursome. Oh, and I must not forget a mother who got away with murder when in her teens, but now her daughter is sweet sixteen and curious to solve the mystery that enfolds her family.

As you can tell by the reviews (go to Amazon), you will either really like or really hate "Under Cover" (based on two reviews only - I would love to see more). Oddly enough, both reviews hit the nail on the head. These women are meant to be humorous - characterizations whose experiences are so extreme as to dare You to laugh.

Since then I have had Create Space print a small book about how friendships grew as seven women met with needles in hand to create quilts. "Stitching Together" is based on the twenty-five years since that first meeting and a group that has grown from seven quilters to over fifty members. We have raised thousands of dollars for breast cancer research through quilt auctions and have given quilts to women and children in hospitals, early birthed babies, persons in safe houses for the abused, food pantries and fire departments, libraries and organizations including parent teacher and boys and girls club. "Stitching Together" includes a few pictures of our quilts.

Yes, the fictionalized men, women and children who people my stories move into my brain and become people I know well and with whom I share hopes and goals. I try very hard to have them 'live' their story for the reader rather than just 'telling' what happened with and to them. One of the few editors who did respond to my query: John Scognamiglio, Editor-in-Chief, Kensington Press, called this to my attention. I found it easy to do, and a lot more fun. John, receiving your brief input made all the time I spent writing to editors and agents worthwhile - like a gem found in the vacuum bag.

    The characters in "Johanna" are not real or based on specific individuals living or dead. They are fictional personalities living in Europe and/or America in the early part of the twentieth century. The historical aspects are a background for my characters' actions. In 1911 a number of Albanian immigrants did settle in the Bronx. The Titanic did sink. People in London and New York City did sometimes find transport in Hanson cabs. There were two Balkan wars almost back to back, just months before the outbreak of WWI. A large number of people crossed the Atlantic on steamboats and there were quite a few among them who did die of measles. These and other events of the time covered by this novel were carefully researched and my imagined friends were given this world for their time; this Zeitgeist within which to flourish or flounder. I hope you enjoy traveling back to that era with them and find this trip a highlight in your busy week.
            Merry Reading,
            Mary Jo

JOHANNA

ACKNOWLEDGMENTS

    A large number of marvelous people have helped me since I began this process. My daughter, Donna Hodge, has spent hours working on spacing, spelling and punctuation. She also has read aloud with me - and sometimes silently as we go through chapter by chapter. Her patient encouragement is never missing even when I change a few words and she has to edit again. Most of all she has been all that the most professional editors strive for; keeping tabs on recurring names, a whiz at making sure the time lines all fit with historical events, and adding that special touch of gentle suggestions that sometimes enrich; sometimes require second thought.
    My gratitude to my husband, Charles Hodge, is beyond expression. What a great joy our journey through life together has been. To describe to you his daily helpfulness: taking responsibility for the bulk of the cooking, household and garden needs, is in no way adequate. Yes, any time the computer gets annoyed with me Charles comes to the rescue. Yes, at times he reads aloud and types notes I dictate when my eyes are exhausted and my cast of characters are still going full tilt. Yes, his hugs and his eyes filled with love sustain me. To be his partner in life is a most precious gift.
    My Californians - Daughter Holly Hodge and Granddaughter, Áine Banfield, keep me abreast of the activities of millions of women dancing for equality around

the world. They lift up my spirits and never let me doubt what I can do in spite of the clear knowledge that I cannot get away with saying I am middle-aged ever again. In addition they sent me many photographs from which I selected the front cover of "JOHANNA".

My Sister, Nancy Soteres provided me with helpful observations. She also elicited help from a Dean of the University of Tennessee, Chattanooga, Tennessee, John Friedl. A statement he made brings me back time and again to this endeavor.

"You are a wonderful story teller, and I thoroughly enjoyed your work."

Other family members have assisted in various ways even though they have not seen the manuscript. My brother, John B. McKinney, Jr., and I had long telephone discussions almost nightly between the few months when he was diagnosed with cancer and his last days here. Johnny served in active combat in Vietnam as an Air Force officer flying in helicopters with his team behind enemy lines to rescue the injured and/or stranded. As this was a period when I was doing research and rewrites our conversation frequently included discussion of our novels in progress.

Others who provided feedback include: Lorraine Ludwig, Hamburg, New York; Cynthia Gates, Katie Sturm, Julie Violanti, Sheila Landon, Danielle Gabel and Barbara Brandt of Eden, New York; Debbie Guckes of Denver, Colorado and Tammy Sherwood, Springville, New York. Thanks to all of you for contributing your time and encouragement.

Harvey Stanbrough, Freelance Editor, Author and Poet edited a version of the full novel, called "Cloak of Destiny" and made helpful suggestions.

Thanks to all of you.

JOHANNA

CHAPTER ONE
THE RELUCTANT DEBUTANTE
London, England
1911

"No. No! You will not make me do it. I'll pick my own husband in my own time. What kind of father are you? If you just are tired of me and want me out of the house, send me to school."

"Calm down, Johanna." Franklin Bennett was not handling this well. His daughter was only seventeen. It was beyond him why his wife, Sybil, was so insistent that his daughter's beauty would fade in another year of courting frenzy, as he liked to consider the London 'Season'.

"Your mother believes your schooling is a great deal of the problem. She points out that I've had you reading a wide selection of classics, as well insisting on a good deal more tutors and schooling than is proper for a young lady."

"Yes, bring up Mother. By all means. You and I both know she is behind all this rush. Goodness knows why. She had me come out last year for all the parties she wanted to attend. Now we've repeated all this nonsense. I personally cannot stand it."

"Your mother has a responsibility to you to see that you are married to the proper person. She has cared for you all these years and cannot stop until you are settled."

"How can you say that, Father? Your sister, Aunt Betsy, spent more time with me than Mother, coming here or taking me to her home while Mother roamed the Continent. What was it when I was three? Oh, yes, the Safari.

"I hope to travel, also, but before I marry and have

children."

"Your mother had a nervous condition. Winters were harsh for her." Franklin admitted, wondering who this emerging woman was standing in front of him. She had grown up from the little girl with whom he occasionally took the time to discuss a book. Yes, he had even read aloud with her once or twice. Now she was no longer the little girl who could be distracted with a bit of candy.

The girl staring at him was on the verge of screaming.

"I only wish Mother would be reasonable. She could be my travel companion. Has your sister approached you about this? Aunt Betsy wants to go with me and the fortune Grandmother left me will more than take care of both of us without any contribution from you."

"Daughter, you are not hearing me. You have until the end of the week to chose a husband or I will pick for you. There are eight names in this envelop. Before we leave here next weekend for the Duke's house party, you are to give me the list with all names crossed off, save one. Your mother and I will announce the engagement just before the dancing begins. Sybil and I are of one accord on this and you are seventeen and under our protection."

"This is unfair and unworthy of you, Father. At least I suddenly understand the rush. Well, announce what you please. I'll delay the marriage until after I am eighteen if I have to get with child by the butcher to do so. Then the trust fund will be accessible to me and me alone."

"Johanna! You have never spoken to me in this manner. You know Sybil and I have your best interests in mind. As she points out having your children grow up with entitlements will give them a great advantage in life. I see that aspect, but even more important, your oldest son could become a member of the landed gentry. If you are wise in choosing among the eight, he could inherit quite a bit of land."

Johanna looked down at her hand holding the envelope. Quicky she ripped it in two; then ripped it again, throwing

JOHANNA

the pieces on the floor in front of her startled father. She stormed out of the room and up the stairs.

Not waiting for her maid to assist with a careful removal of the night's expensive gown, Johanna pulled at the tiny buttons. Several snapped enabling the angry girl to throw the ball gown on the floor. Free of one garment, she struggled with her petticoats. Her boned corset was pinching her back. She discarded it and the other unnameable garments.

"Undoubtedly a man designed these corsets; probably originally to use in torture chambers," she muttered. Johanna breathed a great sigh of relief now that all the laces that had pulled her waist to its tiniest were undone and lying on the floor next to the ball gown. Johanna chose a fresh night gown from her wardrobe. She began to braid her hair so that it would not tangle as she slept. There was another exhausting party tomorrow.

Well, I'll just not go, Johanna thought. They can announce that I'm marrying the man in the moon, but I'll have a fainting spell or slip out the back door.

Johanna's mother, Sybil, floated into the room, still wearing her ball gown of blue, matching her eyes.

"Oh, oh dear, I hope you found someone tonight," she said. "Three gentlemen have asked your father for your hand. I hope one of these three is suitable to you. Certainly, the Earl is very handsome."

So, she is going to play the game of 'I have no idea why your father called you to meet in the drawing room.' I can play that game, too. Johanna barely hid her smirk.

"Oh, Mother, why do you always want to push me to decide. Frankly I don't want any of these men. They cannot see past their own noses. They drive around in carriages all day unless they have those noisy new motor vehicles that frighten the horses. All they want to talk about are golf and tennis and horses and hunting. I don't think a single one of them ever reads a book."

"When you're young it's the time to enjoy life, not sit at home and read books. The gentlemen go to clubs and play cards to establish business connections that later will help them make it in the world," her mother said. "Franklin has his heart set on a title for you and your children."

"Most of the men who come to the parties we've chosen have no plans to ever make it in the world. They plan to live on their fathers' and grandfathers' successes, or to marry a rich woman. It's Father's success in banking and stocks that makes me so popular with these dandies. If they knew about the trust fund Grandmommie left me, they would be climbing in my window."

"Even your adoring grandmother wanted a title for you. She harassed me about marrying beneath my station until you arrived. Then she put all her hopes of royalty on you."

Johanna was tired of the conversation. She spat out her next words.

"You married a man who works and you're proud of him; yet you want me to marry a man without an original thought in his head."

"But dear, a title trumps a brain every time in this world we happen to live in. You were raised to stand toe-to-toe with any Princess."

"Oh for heaven sakes, Mother; I'll tell you what. You get a Prince to come to one of these balls. The night he asks for my hand, I'll accept even though I believe the titles mean nothing anymore.

"At any rate I am too young to be sold off in marriage. I want to try to see some of the world. After I marry I'll be obliged to do whatever my husband wants to do. It might be different if I was in love with one of these men, but that's unlikely, considering their total insistence on talking about nothing but themselves.

The door squeaked as Elizabeth joined mother and daughter.

"Welcome, Aunt Betsy," Johanna brightened. "Perhaps you can convince Mother to give up on marrying me off this

JOHANNA

year."

"Hello dear, you did seem bored tonight," Elizabeth answered. She had been staying with Johanna's family lately as she was unable to recover from the sudden death of her husband several years prior.

"Tonight, and last night and tomorrow night," Johanna sighed.

"Well, Johanna, if you haven't done so by now, you're unlikely to choose a husband this season. I'm going to talk to your father about having you come with me on a trip to France and Italy. You could come with us, also, Sybil. It would be fun!"

"You know Franklin. He depends on me to even get out of bed in the morning," said Sybil.

"See what I mean. These men all have the same problem."

Johanna shook her head.

"I'll never get to go and visit any place further away than Dover, if even that. I do so want to go to Paris, Florence and Rome, and I would love to see Madrid and Barcelona. They have such remarkably romantic names."

Elizabeth hugged Johanna.

"Well, if I have anything to do with it you will be traveling with me for a few months. Coming out can wait until next year, when you're more ready for marriage. Meanwhile, send regrets for the party tomorrow night. We're going shopping together for our traveling clothes."

Breakfast the next morning was seething with efforts to be cheerful, mostly led by Aunt Betsy. Franklin finished his scone and sipped the last of his coffee.

"I accepted a proposal of marriage for you late last night. You'll need to send regrets for tonight's party I invited your intended to a family dinner. I want all of you to behave civilly. That includes you, Johanna!"

"You accepted!" Johanna said. "I thought the idea was for me to choose."

"Yes, and you had your chance. You have rejected over half of the season's best catches. Obviously, you don't know what is for your own good! Actually, I am glad you were so particular. This one is worth the wait!"

"So, who is this 'perfect' match?"

"You'll find out at dinner." Franklin walked out the door, heading to his office.

The three women hesitated to give up their plan for shopping: the perfect antidote for anxiously awaiting the presence of the 'perfect suitor.' Elizabeth drew Sybil aside.

"Don't suggest things for Johanna to try today. Give her complete freedom to make her own selections. She is ripe for a battle."

"I have no intention of choosing for her. Sometimes I must at least protest, especially her choice in hats." Sybil countered.

JOHANNA

CHAPTER TWO
DECISIONS
Western Europe

Aunt Betsy was looking forward to dinner. She had noticed a certain man in private discussion with Franklin late the night before. In fact she was more delighted than anytime since her husband, Thomas, an avid horseman, took one jump too many. If indeed this was the man that Franklin had chosen for Johanna, she would at least get opportunities to enjoy his company.

Dinnertime came all too quickly for Johanna who was hardly in any mood to be sociable. However, she was curious as to who among the empty-headed bachelors her father thought so outstanding. The rest of the family was in the library when she descended the stairs.

"My dear! We were about to call you," Franklin said. "You remember the Viscount, Lawrence Simmons?"

"Of course," Johanna met him halfway across the room. He took her hand and bowed.

This is odd, Johanna thought. This man is father's age! I never considered him to even be one of the options.

At dinner the Viscount was seated next to Johanna, with Elizabeth facing them across the wide table. Johanna had danced with the Viscount on several occasions, but had never spoken to him at any length. She was so taken aback she did not fathom what they could chat about. Elizabeth stepped in with her best charming manner.

"What brings you to England? Is your work in India at an end?"

"The talk of war, I fear! Over the past month there have

been high level talks. My observations about events in India were requested." He turned toward Johanna. "Now I have six weeks left of my leave. I hope you will return with me when that time is up, Miss Bennett."

This man wastes no time in formalities and small talk, thought Johanna. He expects me to *live* in India!

"For how long does your post in India continue," asked Sybil.

"Seven years." The Viscount continued to address Johanna. "I think you will like it there. Your maturity and interest in the world were the characteristics that first attracted me to you. Some of the debutantes are - well, vacuous, for lack of a better word. I will truly enjoy showing you the highlights of India - the art and the architecture alone will delight you."

"Sir, this is all so sudden. We've not had any time to get acquainted!" Johanna tried to keep her voice calm.

"Let's start by how we'll address one another. I prefer Lawrence and Johanna, if that pleases you. The formal Lord and Lady Simmons will do if you prefer."

Johanna broke out in nervous laughter!

"Responding to 'Lady Simmons' will take some getting use to," she said, noticing that no one else was laughing.

The maid interrupted the silence that followed, bringing the entree. Elizabeth took up the slack.

"I hear you are writing a travel manual about India, Viscount!"

Now the Viscount laughed.

"Writing is probably not a good word for it. I am taking pictures wherever I go and jotting down descriptions of what I've seen of the splendor of India. I also collect information about some of the poverty and squalor."

"Tell us, what is the most splendid..."

Johanna found she could not listen, almost choking on her duck! Later she found herself alone with the Viscount.

JOHANNA

"Your Aunt Elizabeth and I were just talking. It seems this has all been sprung on you too quickly. She has suggested that I join the two of you in your travels, at least as far as Paris and Rome. That will give us an opportunity to get acquainted. If you will have my hand in marriage, we will make plans for a simple wedding just before my return to India."

"Like putting the honeymoon in front of the vows," Johanna said.

"Rather. But whether the marriage bed is in Italy or India is entirely up to you."

"That is kind of you. However, I must know. Do you love me?"

"As you pointed out at dinner, I hardly know you enough for such intense emotions. My sons from my first marriage are adventurers, scattered all over the world. My wife died of pneumonia over three years ago. I am a very lonely man and you are well-read and think for yourself. I had an arranged marriage before. Susan and I met on our wedding day. Over time our love developed. I think we have to start with respect and I have that for you. At my age I don't know if love will come again, but I will settle for intelligent companionship."

"That sounds like a beginning and I would love to see India. However, I cannot imagine how a marriage would work without love. In spite of my father's choosing for me, will you accept the fact that I won't decide until I know you better. If you want my respect, I must be given an option to say 'No'."

The Viscount sighed. "I only have six weeks left; then I have no choice but to return to India. I don't have an alternate mate in mind, in spite of all the parties. I will agree to await your decision, but only for three weeks. Then we must talk again. If you have not decided in my favor, that will give me little time to find a wife. But I am willing to make that compromise. I do want this marriage to last if it occurs at all."

"Then as soon as we have spent a few days traveling, I will tell you my decision. I'll try to make it less than two weeks."

JOHANNA

CHAPTER THREE
EYES WIDE OPEN
Paris, France

 Johanna was so excited the day they left, she could hardly contain herself. She had always been the excitable type; jumping up and down over Christmas trees and Easter bunnies, and even the most mundane of daily events. The girl loved books about far away places and at last she was going to see some of the special landmarks she had read about, beginning in Paris.

 As a matter of fact, the only thing that Sybil had ever seen Johanna not excited about was a husband. Her daughter's departure was far from exciting for Sybil.

 "See what you've done," Sybil yelled at Franklin.

 "I should be the one chaperoning our daughter, not your sister. I tell you no good will come of this."

 "You were invited. Now that they have made accommodations for three, it is a little late to decide you want to go."

 "Elizabeth could stay here and take care of you. If you insisted she would have no choice other than to do what you asked."

 "They are leaving today, wife. The Viscount can afford no delays and you would need weeks to assemble your wardrobe, not to mention your travel documents. Let's try to be cheerful. You can start planning the wedding and a trip to India to visit our daughter and her groom."

 "That's yet another problem. Our grandchildren will be so far away we won't even know them. Your insistence that our only child receive a good education has left us with a daughter that the best mates avoid. Johanna is much better read than most men. Many are intimidated by Johanna. She refuses to give them a chance to get to know her. The only reason they court her is your money and I expect one or two know that she received a fortune from my doting Mother."

Sybil married beneath herself, in Johanna's grandmother's opinion. Nevertheless, once Johanna was born, her grandmother had nothing but love for the baby. She spent all the time she could with Johanna. In her will she left all of her estate in trust to Johanna, arguing that Sybil and Franklin really didn't need any more money due to Franklin's business astuteness. Indeed, the reason Sybil's mother had so much money to leave to Johanna was because she listened to Franklin's advise regarding her investments.

Paris was all Johanna had expected! The art galleries were beyond inspiring. She couldn't decide if she preferred more time in the galleries or in sections of the city where young, yet unknown, artists worked their magic on the sidewalks and in the parks.

Johanna's stamina proved much superior to her companions. They encouraged Johanna to linger as long as she liked in a favorite cathedral or exceptional museum. She did so willingly, relishing the time exploring many attractions she had read about. With only two weeks in Paris, she wanted every minute possible filled with the wonders the city had to offer.

Impressed by the Palais du Luxembourg, Johanna delighted even more at the children wading in the lake in front of the palace. She felt she could spend the entire afternoon just watching the little ones sail their boats - some expensive toys; some made with scraps of paper.

So enamored was Johanna of all the beauty to behold, it was well into the second week before she suspected what

JOHANNA

was happening between her two traveling companions. One day she rounded a corner heading for a sidewalk café. Steps away, she saw her Aunt and the Viscount seated at one of the small tables, leaning toward one another, seemingly unaware of the world around them. Another evening she watched in wonder as they danced. There was definitely a spring in Aunt Betsy's step that Johanna had never seen before.

She's truly happy, Johanna realized.

By the time they prepared to leave Paris, Johanna was certain. Elizabeth would be the one going to India with the Viscount. If they were not aware of how suited they were for each other, she would need to help them open their eyes.

I should have seen it from that first dinner, Johanna thought. That night my aunt was smitten either by his manner or his title - perhaps even earlier at one of the parties.

"We have an hour before the train leaves," Johanna said, after the bags were on the way downstairs, carried by porters. "Could we all sit down and discuss our future plans."

"That would please me," the Viscount said.

Johanna began with her softest voice.

"Love is something that sometimes develops over years, especially between two people who have a lot in common. At other times it sneaks up quickly, and is hardly recognized by those it entangles. I have enjoyed this trip with both of you so far. Viscount, you are a most gracious traveling companion. However, I don't see myself sitting alone in a strange country while my husband works, and making small talk with women who have had life experiences very different than mine. That is more Aunt Elizabeth's cup of tea."

"Oh, dear, I would be happy to go with you - of course if it is alright with Larry."

"It would be my pleasure, Bess; two lovely companions instead of one."

Johanna interrupted.

"I have heard love is blind, so I must be your eyes, as the Viscount has little time. How can I say it? I have never seen two people more in love with each other. Look into your hearts and you will see it. The comfort you have with each other. The smiles when you accidently touch! The way you sometimes start to say the same thing at the same time."

Elizabeth put out her hand, as if to hush Johanna. But Johanna ignored the signal.

"No, say nothing now. When we board the train I am taking my book to the club car while you two spend some time together in our compartment. Then when we meet again tell me that I'm not right in my observations or let's end this charade and plan your elopement!"

JOHANNA

CHAPTER FOUR
WHEN IN ROME
Italy

In Rome, Elizabeth rented a Villa in a quiet section of the city.

"A cook comes with this Villa, so we won't have to worry about food. We can eat out when we like or have our meals served here." Elizabeth said. Then, noting there were two large bedrooms, one located in a loft just above the kitchen and parlor, she continued.

"You take the loft, dear, at your age these stairs will not be a challenge. Larry and I will share the lower bedroom."

The Villa was indeed charming with a patio, garden, kitchen with a corner nook for meals and a small library. All were furnished in the Tuscany style.

The Viscount made arrangements for a car and driver to be at their disposal afternoons and evenings. Johanna rented a bicycle from the cook's son, and explored on her own in the mornings, being careful to count out streets and to make a circle tour, each day widening the circle.

"I am in love with Rome. I never want to leave," Johanna confessed to the chauffeur, Antonio. "You have been a great tour guide."

Antonio spoke English as well as Italian and added a merry, fun element to their outings. More often than not he became Johanna's escort at the theater or nightclub since the two 'lovebirds', as she had come to think of them, pleaded excuses to return to the Villa.

"Your aunt and the Viscount remind me of couples I escort on their honeymoons," Antonio observed. He and

Johanna had spent the morning looking for the perfect small chapel for a private wedding. "When I first started as your driver I thought you were to marry this man."

"Oh, no. That changed in Paris. Elizabeth and Lawrence were destined for each other. They just needed a little help realizing this."

The special day arrived. Johanna brushed Elizabeth's hair and coaxed it into a half-circle coiffure; then placed a circlet of lily-of-the-valley neatly above the resulting updo.

"The white suit was the perfect choice," Johanna remarked. "Also, the lacy blouse. Either will look wonderful when you join Larry at the altar, and you can decide on adding the jacket at the last minute depending on the weather. You have a bouquet of large white calla lilies waiting for you at the chapel. They will complement the tiny lilies I just put in your hair. Also, I used the same lilies in the decorations for the altar. Now, I have a surprise for you."

Elizabeth carefully opened the small box that Johanna handed her. Upon seeing the contents, she sighed deeply, a tear dropping from one eye. The bracelet featured individual stones of London blue topaz - the darker, richer color of blue than the more common topaz. The stones were set in sterling silver.

"My Grandmother once told me that when I marry I should be sure to have something old, something new, something borrowed and something blue. When she went away from our sight this was among her jewels. I want you to 'borrow' it for the rest of your time on earth. Then you will have something old that is new to you, and definitely, something blue."

"Have a great trip to Sicily," Johanna called, as Betsy and Larry boarded the train. "I'll send a telegram to Mother and Father, informing them of the nuptials. Then when you get back to London they will have had time to absorb the news of your marriage. Write me in care of Cook when you get to India."

JOHANNA

There was only a short time left in the Viscount's vacation. Planning the trip to India was time consuming. Most of the clothes suitable for the Indian climate would best be purchased there. However, there was the issue of Elizabeth's house. The newly-wed couple decided to spend a few days in Sicily; then return to England to complete arrangements there. They gave Johanna the choice of accompanying them or employing the cook as a companion if she wished to stay in Rome.

Of course Johanna chose the latter. She had planned to travel on to Florence - part of the original itinerary. However, she never wanted to leave Rome. As soon as the decision was made for the new couple to leave, Johanna contacted a realtor and began looking at villas for sale.

Johanna brushed her thick chestnut hair until it glistened. She put on her blue flowered sun dress, tossing aside the conservative jacket that was made for it. Then she applied her make-up and perfumes as carefully as if going to an English ball. Antonio was escorting her to the opera tonight. They had spent the day walking among the ancient ruins of the coliseum. Before leaving for the long outing she chose a silver opera bag and high-heels and her satin, dress-length opera coat - all to leave in the car until evening.

Johanna realized she was entranced not only with Rome, but with Antonio. Perhaps they seemed one and the same to her. Each evening when alone they enjoyed the night-life of Rome and the romance of walking through the streets. The lantern lights gave the aura of moonlight, with a moon on every corner. Antonio was a perfect escort; incredibly attentive and considerate and also full of pleasant stories about each place they visited. He questioned her about her favorite books and music and took her dancing under the stars where outdoor bands seemed never to tire of making music.

"I'm thinking of buying a villa here. This has been so much fun, I can't bear leaving! I actually have one in mind that I've been visiting mornings on my bike."

Antonio had parked and they were walking toward the outdoor dance floor.

"Of course I might not live here full time, but I think the cook we have now will keep it clean for me and her son will do the gardening. Then I can return whenever it pleases me."

"Would your aunt be willing to help you finance such a plan?" Antonio asked.

"Oh, no need for that! I've scarcely spent anything from my trust fund. A couple of months savings from that should be more than adequate for the first payment at least."

"Then - wonderful!" Antonio was taken aback. "I will only be available evenings, however. I've used my two weeks vacation."

"You are so skilled at this - I thought it was what you did all the time."

"Only weekends and vacations. I'm saving to travel also. My regular job is with a law firm."

They reached the dance floor; the band was playing a waltz.

"May I have this dance?" he asked gallantly, taking her hand and kissing it gently.

The next morning Antonio appeared early with a bicycle affixed to the car's fender. He had on pants that just covered his knees and a sleeveless shirt. On it was an embroidered logo of a local university. The muscles in his arms and legs were the first things she noticed and her heart did a flip flop. She'd never seen a man so close to naked before. All those that came calling wore vested suits and ruffled starched shirts, usually with ascots at their necks. Never had she seen so much of the body of a man. As she watched him whiz by her at the top of the hill, she looked over her shoulder. He brought his bicycle to a quick stop in front of a picturesque villa with a sale sign in front.

"Is this the one you like?" Antonio asked.

"It is nice but my favorite is a block ahead with gardens

JOHANNA

in front and back."

This man on the bicycle was all Italian - jet black hair, mustache and muscles like she had never noticed on an Englishman. Johanna felt a shiver when he took her arm as they walked around to the back garden.

"I want to see the inside," he said, as they circled the back garden. Then he did something so daring it made Johanna's heart race.

"What are you doing? That door is locked!" she gasped. As quickly as he had brought it to his hand, the little pocket knife disappeared and the door swung open.

"We can't go in." Johanna protested.

"Why not? The villa is for sale and you are an interested buyer."

As he spoke he swept her up in his arms, cradling her. Antonio carried her gently through the kitchen and small breakfast nook. At the stairway he shifted her weight, tossing the girl easily over one shoulder. Johanna felt a loss of control with the inability to make eye contact from this position. How can I be angry and excited at the same time, Johanna thought.

Before she could find words to complain they reached the top of the stairs and entered a large bedroom. It was fully furnished and as neat as the kitchen.

"Let's pretend we live here as you have been doing on your bicycle rides. Today we can pretend together. Believe me it is not much fun to live alone. I've tried it for too long."

Laying the dazed girl on the bed and kneeling beside her, Antonio waved his arms in the air, gesturing as if conducting an orchestra. He sang loudly in a deep throaty tone, courting Johanna with his best rendition of an Italian love song.

"May I have this dance?" he asked gallantly, taking her hand and kissing it gently. A part of Johanna cautioned her that this was madness. For one thing she might never see him again. If not very careful she could end up with an unexplainable 'souvenir'.

"The heat is stifling in here," Antonio observed in a husky voice. As he spoke he pulled his shirt over his head.

Johanna abandoned all misgivings. She was amazed as much by the unusual sound of her voice as by the words she was whispering.

"Your muscles; they're so incredible. May I touch them?"

"All you like," Antonio grinned.

Moments later he added, "Now it's my turn." His finger tips brushed her shoulder. He pulled her peasant blouse off one shoulder and quickly freed an ample breast.

"Ah, yes, how perfect," Antonio sighed. "We should have brought wine; a good wine becomes a great wine, enhanced when sipped from a woman's beauty."

Johanna felt she must stop him and soon, but she could hardly catch her breath. As he tasted with his tongue, his hands were busy unfastening first her skirt and then her under things.

"Please," some inner part of Johanna pleaded, even as the sensations caused by his talented tongue and teeth overwhelmed her.

Deep from his throat Antonio answered.

"Please? The other side? Of course, in due time. First, however, I must taste inside of you. Today this is only for you. It is to give you pleasure with no worry that you risk your virginity."

Johanna went completely limp when he moved his tongue down to torment her lower lips, her unused passage, her very soul. Never before had she even imagined such sensations.

Later he brought water from the kitchen pump and bathed and dressed her. She was so spent that he had to carry her back to the garden where he dropped to one knee and proposed. She knew this was too quick; too impulsive, but she was still trembling from the joyous sensations her body had just learned. No Englishman would ever make her feel this way; she was sure of it.

"Yes, Antonio, oh yes," came her answer.

JOHANNA

CHAPTER FIVE
TO LOVE AND OBEY
1911-1912

Johanna planned to have the wedding in London and wrote her parents asking input for an appropriate time. The lease on the villa was expiring soon.

I'll go home and help Mama plan the wedding, Johanna thought. That evening she approached Antonio with the idea.

"My Carissima, my passion for you is such that I cannot bear to be away from you another day; certainly not the weeks you are suggesting. If continuing to stay at this villa is problematic, I can share my apartment with you until we find something more permanent. That is probably a better idea anyway."

"My parents would never approve," Johanna mused.

"Then let's not tell them. Let's elope this next weekend. We can rent a car and drive down to the ocean. We can have a beautiful three days and nights without all the hustle and bustle of a formal wedding. It will be glorious like your aunt's wedding."

"I'll think about it," Johanna said.

"Think while I make love with you," Antonio replied. "Think how it will be to spend entire nights together. Think how it will be skin-to-skin, while I kiss and caress every inch of your lovely body."

Taking her in his arms Antonio took her upstairs to her bed. He made quick work of his unneeded clothing. Then he slowed down as one by one he took off every item of Johanna's clothing, starting with her shoes. He gently caressed her stockinged feet; then walked his nimble fingers up her left leg, removing her garter and slipping her stocking slowly down inch by inch, kissing and nibbling all the way down.

Instead of going directly to her right leg, Antonio straddled the girl, placing the bared leg over his shoulder and nibbling closer and closer to the juncture of her legs, skipping from her flesh above her garter on her right leg, back across nibbling through her drawers at the essential spots to bring her to exquisite agony. By the time he had fully undressed her she was frantic with desire. This time he took her fully, thrusting within her as she breathed heavily and responded by giving as well as receiving. Her hips caught his rhythm as he pushed deeper and deeper. Suddenly, Johanna screamed.

"It is all right, dear Johanna. It won't hurt ever again. You are properly deflowered and open to me now for all time. Bear with me a few moments and then I'll bathe you and brush your beautiful hair."

Once again Johanna lifted her hips to her lover. As he reached his peak she felt an unbelievable power. She'd never dreamed she could assist a man in reaching such heights - indeed she never even imagined another human being in such ecstasy.

Antonio and Johanna were married the day before her lease expired. Still in her teens, Johanna did not question Antonio's rush to the altar. She was proud of her choice to elope. It saved all the verbal warfare. Writing to her parents she imagined their reaction. Mother had wanted her to be a countess or a duchess, even. Father had wanted stability, land, and grandsons. She knew they would be disappointed. But Johanna felt the pressure they put on her to marry someone she didn't even like justified her actions.

This way I get to choose my own husband, she thought.

However, after the first few weeks of their marriage Johanna became bored.

JOHANNA

"Let's have a honeymoon and we can go to London." She approached Antonio as they sat down to the evening meal prepared by the same cook she and her aunt had employed during their stay in Rome.

"I want my parents to meet you and see what a special man I married," she began.

"Let's give them time to get use to the idea of you with an Italian husband before they actually see me. I don't dress the way the English chaps do and I certainly have never been to anything like a debutante ball."

"But Antonio! They are my parents. You will father their grandchildren. The sooner they see how charming you are, the better."

"Do they control your trust fund?"

"No, not really. Father has advised me on major expenditures of which I've only had one - the trip with my Aunt Elizabeth. However, I receive a check directly each month from the bank which touches only the interests on the trust. This goes into an account I can draw from. If I need more I can send a notarized request and monies will be taken from the major account. Otherwise, the amount of the trust is secure and earning the best return possible."

"Do you trust the bank? What if things go bad? Are you certain it is secure? Perhaps you should put it in two or three different places."

"Like where? Under the mattress? It is quite safe in the bank. Soon, I will purchase a villa and we can move out of your apartment. It may have been perfect for you, but most of my gowns are still packed and there is no place for the trunks."

"I will see about getting rid of some old things and giving you an entire wardrobe. Let's not worry about these things tonight You have a husband now and we can make financial decisions together. Soon you can show me what records you keep. Then we can plan our travels. Have you ever thought of going to America?"

"No, but if you like I can read some about it in the

library a few blocks from the old villa. Also, I was thinking of asking the cook to teach me a few of her favorite dishes. I have lots of time now. I've been doing the recommended tours for several weeks. I am going to the library soon and look for information on lesser known archaeological sites."

Finishing his dinner, Antonio arose.

"I've been sitting at a desk all day. I'll just take the bike and go for a short ride while you straighten up from our meal. Then we'll put on some music and dance for a while or you can sing to me. I do already miss the piano in the villa you rented."

Weeks went by and Antonio spent less and less time at home. Johanna's parents' letters came regularly, insistent that they visit. She begged Antonio to go but he made excuse after excuse. At first it was because he had used his vacation time serving as a tour guide when they met. Secretly, Antonio longed to go to America. This had been his dream before meeting Johanna. He resented the large salaries his employers received compared to the small pittance that made up his weekly wage.

Antonio did much of the research for the legal office in which he labored day after day. He was charged with looking up legal precedents and doing most of the searches for and interviews of the potential witnesses.

"In America I will set up my own law office," declared Antonio, as he practiced how he would explain this to Johanna. She was in love with Rome - still not over her initial fascination. It was with great difficulty that he had persuaded her to forego her plan to buy a villa. She was going to argue with him endlessly about emigrating to America, like she had done regarding the purchase of the house. Then she had stomped her foot and shouted until he pointed out that this money she kept speaking about was no longer 'hers'.

"It is 'our' money now that we are wed and I refuse to sign off on a sale of such an expensive item when you have

JOHANNA

only looked at two of at least fifty options."

Yes, she will try every little trick she knows including avoiding my bed. Well, her loss. I have another option in that department just a bicycle ride away.

His thoughts were rambling now, anticipating Johanna's reaction.

I should never have told her I had no law degree; no papers. If we go to one of the frontier towns where there are few if any lawyers it will not matter. Certainly I am knowledgeable, having done much of the legal work here for four years.

Johanna can even assist me. She reads and speaks English much better than me even though I have studied the language for years. Perhaps I should tell her I really need her. I thought when we married that I was so lucky to have met Johanna. She could be a great asset in America as she speaks both French and Italian. My English has improved daily since our marriage, partly because of her daily subscription to the London Times and several magazines published in England.

Oh, and I can't forget the money. She has a reliable income from her trust fund. Not a high income probably, but hopefully one which would enable us to move up my plan to cross the ocean by a good five years. The sooner the better, and a trip to England would be a waste of money, delaying our exodus.

He had not counted on Johanna's stubborn, English resistance! She was elusive with respect to sharing the details of her trust fund, saying that most of the records were in England. Who would ever bring such valuables on a pleasure trip. They could discuss it with a banker when they visited London. Antonio felt that his wife had too much of a mind of her own; her parents had not emphasized the place of a woman in a home, otherwise Johanna would not be still thinking of her money as her own.

"I'll wait until we are aboard a ship to America before I insist on my legal standing," he announced to the mirror as he finish his careful attention to his short beard. "As soon as we arrive in America we will transfer the trust correspondence and other papers to my name."

JOHANNA

CHAPTER SIX
CONFLICTING EXPECTATIONS
Rome, Italy
1912

It should have been a wonderful evening! Johanna had great news. She made a special dinner, following the recipes and techniques she had so recently learned from her Italian cook. She purchased an expensive wine which Antonio had recommended at four of the restaurants when dining with Aunt Betsy and the Viscount.

"You shouldn't have opened this! We could have returned it," Antonio shouted when he saw what she was pouring in his glass.

"We really don't have to scrimp so," Johanna replied. "Besides, I have a surprise for you."

"I hope it is not expensive," her husband growled.

"Well, it could be, but well worth it! We are having a baby. I called the realtor about 'our Villa'. It was sold months ago, but she wants to show us another one, closer to your work. It even has a fenced garden where a child can play."

Antonio rose and took Johanna in his arms. He was delighted about the baby. He believed that a child born on American soil automatically became an American citizen. The parents would be assured of not being extradited.

"When is the baby due? We must prepare at once! Booking passage with all this talk of war is difficult," Antonio announced.

"Passage? Oh, you mean across the Channel! My parents will be delighted!" Johanna smiled.

"The Channel? Of course not! There is no time to go to England. We must try to leave within the fortnight!"

"I don't understand? Where are we visiting!" Johanna asked.

"We're not 'visiting' anyplace! We're emigrating - to America of course! I've dreamed about it for years. We're just moving the time up a few months because of the baby and the possible war!"

"You can't be serious! I knew you wanted to go to America, but not to live! You know how I love Rome!"

"Will you still love it when I am ordered to serve in the Military? How about when the guns are turned on Italy? Even if there was no war coming, do you expect me to slave over old hand-written law books until I go blind? Never will the partners give me a chance in court - even to observe! In American I can have my own practice," Antonio spit out angrily.

"But we have plenty of money! You could quit," Johanna began.

"What kind of man do you think I am? I'll not let my wife support me!"

Antonio burst out the door, slamming it! The special dinner sat on the table turning cold!

Johanna had a restless night. Why had she married so abruptly? Antonio apparently did not come home all night; at least there was no sign of him.

Johanna was annoyed with herself. Why did I marry at all? The monthly checks from the trust faithfully were posted from the bank in England. When they arrived Antonio insisted on taking most for savings. Johanna knew her new status as wife left her little leeway with the legal system. Antonio argued they were now a couple and he was responsible financially for his wife and himself and the children that they might have. Therefore it was his responsibility to plan for the future and take care of the finances.

Johanna had read about tourist spots in America earlier

JOHANNA

in her marriage. She wasn't impressed. Everything was so new. She still had not covered all the places she wanted to visit in Europe - ancient burial grounds in Scotland; the monasteries in Northern Greece and Albania. With a deep sigh Johanna dressed and took her bicycle to research transports available for travel to America.

She had no spirit for the work until the librarian brought her a brochure advertising a new tourists' vessel. This was not your ordinary transit ship but it was a ship to be marveled at – a ship in every sense of the word. It was one of three luxury transports operated by the White Line out of Britain. It was due to sail from London on April tenth.

How perfect, Johanna thought. We can go a few days early. Antonio can meet my parents and we will still get to America in mid-April. At least that is the projection. Some of the ships take several weeks to cross according to the information I've seen today. That this one should only take two weeks is a miracle.

When Antonio got home Johanna approached him joyously.

"I was in the library most of the day researching ships and guess what I found; it's a wonder."

"Unless it's called the Matilda I don't want to hear about it. We're booked and paid for – the ship leaves the beginning of February. We start packing tonight."

"Why do we need to leave so quickly?"

"I told you the baby needs to be born in America; it's essential."

"But the baby is not due until May. Best of all this ship leaves out of London. You can meet my parents and spend a little time with them before we leave for America. It might be years before we can return. I almost wired my father today, but I waited in case you wanted to add something."

"Johanna we're not going to England. We are going to America and the sooner the better. Forget about this visit to your parents. When the baby comes they will probably want to come to America to see the baby anyway. That is if they can get transport out of Europe by that time. The news of war is grave. If we wait another month to leave here I'll most likely be going in the Army, or worse, the Navy. Is that what you want? Then you can take our baby to England to your precious parents and knit socks at night to keep my feet warm."

As Antonio spoke he became more and more excited. He began flinging pillows across the room; then more fragile things, breaking vases and scattering their floral contents.

"We won't need this or this or this," he shouted. "Start packing, Johanna, NOW or do I have to slap you around?"

Johanna dashed for the bathroom saying, "I'll start in here." She locked the door hoping he would calm down when she was out of sight. After a few minutes of yelling she heard the outside door slam and all was quiet.

When Johanna woke the next morning she heard whistling in the kitchen. Three sturdy trunks sat in the middle of the floor in the parlor. Full of resentment Johanna held her tongue. She tried to give Antonio the benefit of the doubt - but she felt he was a coward and a bully. He was afraid of war, she thought. He used a temper tantrum to frighten her into submission. Well, she wasn't humbled; but much of her admiration and respect was turning to resentment. Resentment toward Antonio and absolute anger at her choices since coming to Rome.

Grandmommie would tell me it is time to grow up and THINK before I act. I must make an effort to make this marriage work, especially with the baby I now carry. I'll have to learn from my indulgence. I got even with my parents for pushing me into a loveless marriage in the hope love would come. I found love or what I thought was love and now instead of growing it is like a candle, with such a seductive light, but burning bright no longer.

JOHANNA

CHAPTER SEVEN
ALL ABOARD
On the ship Matilda crossing the Atlantic Ocean
February 1912

The bravery of the emigrants to the New World cannot be questioned. The ocean had to be crossed by the millions who sought a new haven. To step aboard a ship while looking out across the immense ocean must have caused many a heart to flutter. Possibly some turned away, but if any lost courage and gave up their passage, they remain unheralded. Each ship leaving an European port in the years shortly before the outbreak of the first World War held the maximum number of passengers, sometimes more. Each traveler was filled with awe and hope as they stepped aboard.

    Johanna hastily gathered her notes, as they prepared to leave after a restless week waiting for the Matilda. She should have suspected a delay. Ever the young woman who liked to prepare for experiences by reading, she was aware of two types of ships: newer and refitted ships and older ships with no renovations. Often there were substitutions of older ships for the more comfortable refitted or new ships, as the newer vessels were needed as countries prepared for war.
    As Johanna looked up at the Matilda she felt as if a shadow crossed the sun. Never the superstitious type she

brushed the feeling aside. As they got nearer she had to take her eyes off the craft and look out at the calm ocean. This was not a ship to warm the hearts of those traveling.

"She looks old. Are we really booked on this?" Johanna asked in despair.

"It was difficult enough to get passage at all, especially first class which you insisted upon," the impatient Antonio replied gruffly.

"You used to be so cheerful and agreeable. I hope the change of attitude is brought on because of the pregnancy." he added. "Otherwise I have married a shrew. You complain about everything."

It was true. Johanna was out of sorts. She had barely been sleeping. The baby chose the night to kick merrily. Anguish was in her heart.

How has this happened she thought. What brought me here - what forces of nature and poor judgement. I knew if I married I would lose my right to make my own decisions. After taking such care to choose a mate in London, I fell for the first man I met in Rome.

As they boarded the Captain approached Antonio.

"You almost 'missed the boat' literally," the Captain announced. "Two more minutes and I would have given your cabin to a stand-by. We can't afford to wait for late-comers; our schedules are hard to keep up in these days of warmongering!"

Antonio started to put the captain in his place, but Johanna interrupted her husband.

"I'm afraid I have to take the blame, Sir," she sang in her softest voice. "I hope by the time I'm with child again, I will be able to manage carrying it with more agility."

"Of course, I'm just glad you made it. Welcome aboard. You must be tired. Dinner will be at 7:00. If you are rested by then, I hope you will join me at my table."

"That is most gracious of you," Johanna answered, tossing her chestnut curls out of her eyes.

"Send our trunks up right away," Antonio blurted, taking

JOHANNA

Johanna's arm and pushing past the captain.

The first two nights were fun.

"Now that we are on the way to America, we can relax a little," Antonio commented. "My choice of ships is turning out well. I know I chose a ship based on the first available date of departure even though advised that a more modern ship than the Matilda would be available just a few days later. I just had an urgent feeling that we should leave Europe quickly. Now the moon is out and we can walk on this upper deck and just enjoy. I feel young again. We are on our way to my dream."

"Look, the steerage passengers are dancing on the lower deck," Johanna laughed. Someone has a balalaika and they are dancing and singing."

Antonio held out his hand.

"Shall we dance, too?" he offered.

Morning found Johanna back outside. She wandered around the upper deck, enjoying the breeze and the sun. Looking down she saw a lovely woman on the lower deck. The woman was smiling and looking directly at Johanna. Johanna waved her arms then encircled her belly with them. They both laughed. Another with a baby! The woman opened her cloak to show more clearly that she was quite close to birthing.

Johanna reached into her pocket for an orange she had put there earlier. Still laughing she tossed it to the woman below, who caught it easily. What a lovely woman she is, thought Johanna.

The woman blew her a kiss of thank you before Johanna lost sight of her as more people crowded onto the lower deck.

Back in her cabin, Johanna found Antonio awake.
"Good morning."
Her greeting was cheerful in the hope of finding her

husband still in a good mood. "There is another with child on board. I just saw her down on the steerage deck."

"Why should a steerage passenger be of concern to us? The wind has matted your hair. Sit down."

Johanna raised a beguiling eyebrow and loosened the pins left in her thick, curly locks. Antonio picked up the brush and began stroking her richly colored chestnut hair. Once leaving his apartment to travel to their port of departure, he began doing this every morning. Ocean voyages and waiting to board were both so tiresome; there was nothing to do! Now on board, the walls of the small cabin seemed to creep closer and closer. At times he could hardly breathe.

Not only couldn't he breathe, there wasn't room in the cabin for all their trunks. He worried about someone stealing his secret stash of law books carefully secured in a hidden compartment of one of the trunks. It had taken great stealth to relieve his old law office of these books but certainly he deserved them after all his hours laboring for such a measly salary.

Johanna hated putting up with his moods but loved this uncharacteristic attention. She thought Antonio loved her, as she had felt she loved him. However, seldom had he lingered in the home they had shared for the past year. Antonio had typically started his day at a coffeehouse where he met lifelong friends. From there he went straight to the solicitor's office where he was assisting in the city's foremost criminal cases, mostly researching old court papers looking for precedents. Though married he saw no reason to vary this routine.

As he brushed her hair, he once again considered himself lucky to have made her Mrs. Antonio Marino. Johanna was beautiful - full-breasted, hips made for childbearing, perfect teeth and green eyes that could light up a room.

Except for a few nights when she pouted over Villas and steam ships, she responded to his romantic overtures enthusiastically. This was a pleasant surprise as he had always heard English girls were cold in that regard. Certainly not Johanna! If anything, she was little on the wild side.

Of course, now they were putting the amorous part of their life together on hold for the baby that was on the way. The baby must be born in America - on American soil. If this dilapidated tub they called a ship would only hurry, life would be great. As he brushed Johanna's lush tresses he was so sure of that.

Johanna adapted to the sea voyage much better than Antonio. The first rainy days he could not leave the cabin. Even looking at the water made him seasick. Johanna went on deck whenever possible and inhaled deeply the sea air, considering it great for the baby.

She had even found a friend - of sorts. The pregnant girl - younger than she was or so she believed. This girl was confined to the deck below as she was a steerage passenger.

After spotting the young woman the first morning out, Johanna looked for her every day. Johanna had saved another orange from the breakfast that was offered for the first class passengers. Her intention was to toss fruit to the pregnant woman every morning to supplement the diet given the steerage passengers, which she imagined not sufficient for a developing baby.

This only worked twice. On the third morning a tall lad watched as the two waved at each other. When Johanna threw the fruit he jumped up and caught it high in the air before it reached the intended recipient. A seaman noticed and cautioned Johanna that soon dozens would be fighting for her fruit.

"But she is with child. She needs the extra nourishment," Johanna pleaded.

"Those in steerage are a hardy lot. She will be fine for the few days we are at sea."

As Johanna watched, the girl's cloak was suddenly

whipped to the side by a gust of wind.

    She is due soon, Johanna thought. I wonder if we will ever meet. I wish I could throw her a basket of oranges. Even more I wish we could meet somewhere and talk. I am hungry for female company.

JOHANNA

CHAPTER EIGHT
STORM BREWING
Winter on the Atlantic
1912

    The wind grew cold and relentless, causing most of the passengers to remain in their rooms. Those in steerage were a little slower to seek shelter as their accommodations were so meager. With the wind came the rain and it came in torrents. Sheets of water washed up from the ocean to meet the downpour as it fell. Shortly the ship tossed wildly in the angry ocean. No one would have dared go on deck even if it had been allowed. People were losing everything they ate. The overflowing buckets could not accommodate all the waste.
    Antonio huddled in his bed, fully believing he would die at any moment. For two nights and three days the ship tossed in the strong winds. For two nights and three days, Antonio ate nothing and hardly slept.
    On the third night, the ocean calmed. Down in steerage the children that had screamed for what seemed an eternity finally slept. The women who were able cleaned the steerage areas as best they could as the men gathered on the deck and began singing and smoking.
    Antonio was not comforted. The calmness seemed like death to him. The rash he had contracted was driving him mad. He was vaguely aware of Johanna putting wet cloths on his face which he tossed off trying to scratch the persistent itch.

    Johanna watched out the small window as Marco, the

ship's captain paced up and down the upper deck.

Marco was worried. Johanna could clearly hear his loud muttering as he paced back and forth.

"Father should have known better. Just because he is rich and owns a bunch of ships, he thinks he can make me a captain overnight. Well, he can call me that but that doesn't mean I know what to do. To give me a ship like this for my first voyage as captain was insane. Father knew my lack of experience. Why didn't he give me a decent vessel to command and not this old tub? Did he know what a risk he was taking? Or when he heard the Leona II had double the number who wanted passage than she could accommodate, did he just go for the money? Probably I was the only captain left that the Royal Navy had not taken."

"Now we have blown off course and are delayed - who knows for how long. The navigator is in bed with this rash and has such a fever I doubt he knows exactly where we are. Meanwhile, I have six deaths on my hands already, among the very young and very old steerage passengers."

"If it's measles we could have an epidemic. Must be measles from the rashes on the sick. Oh what, oh what was Father thinking. Even the ship's doctor is exhausted just from caring for the passengers in the upper decks. He shows little inclination to complete the required physical exams of those in steerage.

"So many worries. Will the food even last since we are off course? After all, we are overloaded. Why didn't I just turn some away? Instead I had the crew put sleeping berths where a dining area should have been. What a fool I am!"

The captain's plaintive voice was not the only thing to concern Johanna. She trembled as she felt the brow of her fevered husband. She was almost sure the red rash that had appeared was measles; something she had experienced in her youth. Can the baby inside of me catch the measles from Antonio or does my immunity protect it?

JOHANNA

CHAPTER NINE
TRAGEDY
Somewhere on the Atlantic Ocean
Spring 1912

Johanna held her aching stomach, hoping to feel some movement.

"I swear to God I'll never set foot on a sea-going vessel again," Johanna sighed as she looked through the small porthole. "Just please save my baby. She is so tiny. She should still be developing inside me."

Johanna was isolated in this dreary cabin; her last contact from outside was the worrisome words of the young captain. Travel across the great Atlantic brought freedom for some; agony for many. Johanna, though not quite yet out of her teens, felt that her husband of less than a year had made a poor decision. Now Antonio was sick and more was wrong with him than a rash and seasickness. On his last visit the ship's doctor diagnosed him as having measles and quarantined the little cabin. To make matters worse the wind swirled out of the North. By noon, the sky was as dark as night. The ancient ship was tossed terribly by the monstrous waves.

"Will this storm never cease?" Johanna worried aloud.

Meanwhile Antonio lost every drop of food or liquid put into his mouth. As his fever spiked he became delirious, frightening Johanna. He flung his arms wildly, speaking nonsense when he spoke at all. This morning she was in the path of his flailing arm and was knocked across the cabin. By noon her water broke.

Johanna was beside herself. She could not leave the

quarantined cabin to find the doctor. Why had he not come back by now? She had begged him to put Antonio in the sick bay so the baby would be safe. The doctor had flatly refused her request.

"I can't expose every sick person on board to the measles. We already have over eleven cases. I'm only one person and the only physician aboard. I'll stop in again to check on him soon. When did you say your baby was expected?"

The storm's end heralded the doctor's return to find Johanna unconscious and the baby born early and barely alive. Once the doctor revived Johanna, he took papers from his case.

"I have no time for all this paper work. When you fill them out make a copy for me. The birth weight is about four pounds. I'll try to get back before dark."

The baby was too weak to nurse, though Johanna tried. Soon after the doctor left the baby took her last breath. Johanna held the frail child tightly, frozen with grief. Antonio's fate was to join his daughter within the hour. Johanna's world was ending.

"God where are you? Do you not follow us aboard ships? How can this be; I'm not yet twenty and already a widow and my precious child hardly took a breath? Why not take me and let her live? I am a thankless person, with no purpose in life."

An hour later a seaman arrived, sent by the exhausted doctor to see if all was well. He called for help with Johanna's dear ones. The newcomers wrapped Antonio in sheets. Assisted by the others the seaman got Antonio over one shoulder as a younger sailor reached for the baby.

"Where are you taking them?" Johanna screamed. "No, no, not the baby. Is there not a minister of God on board for a small service? My daughter has not even been christened."

"They will be interned at sea. We have had several go

JOHANNA

before them and others likely following soon. There is no sanitary way to keep diseased bodies on board, not even long enough to arrange a service."

"No! I'll not let her go with you!" Johanna screamed.

The seaman spoke quietly as they took the bodies away.

"I think the captain is arranging a joint service for all who have gone from this ship. It will probably be tomorrow morning. Why don't you rest awhile; then write up a poem or something you want to say. Meanwhile, I'll send a young boy recruited from steerage to wash down the walls and clean everything in the cabin.

Johanna was so distraught when they brought clean linens she couldn't even speak. Alone, she cried hysterically. Catching her breath she thought she heard Antonio.

"Antonio, Antonio. Have you come for me? Is God in heaven taking us to his Paradise or is he judging us unworthy? Are you with little Maria? I know how badly you wanted her to be born on American soil, but now you see it does not matter at all.

"Yes, I hear you calling. I'll come right away. Where ever the journey - to Heaven or to hell - I will follow for the sake of our precious baby."

Johanna stepped out of the cabin and looked toward the ocean. The ocean is calling me, she thought. I hear Antonio calling in the wind. I want to join Antonio and my baby. They are in the ocean. I hear them calling me!

Little Maria is crying for me, though the wind drowns out her screams. I must go with them. I MUST; I MUST!

These thoughts and only these plagued Johanna. Still weak from the birth, she stumbled toward the door. Opening it against the insistent wind was no easy task, but Johanna was assisted by her focused determination. She left her cabin with no coat; no shoes even. Her long skirts blew against her legs, making progress difficult. She was shivering from the cold by the time she found a stairway to take her to the lower deck. She had to get to the lower deck and over the side someway.

"Is that you, Mrs. Marino?" she heard a voice call.

She had to follow her family into the sea. Antonio was calling her name. Yes, Antonio was calling her.

"Mrs. Marino? Where are you going. No, don't climb over that railing! Wait, wait - we really need your help."

JOHANNA

CHAPTER TEN
"SOMEONE'S CALLING ME"
Somewhere On The Atlantic Ocean
March 1912

Johanna was confused. Where were her shoes? The wind was blowing so fiercely she could hardly stay upright.

"Antonio is calling me. I must go to him. In the ocean? The seaman was taking him to the ocean. But I hear him calling me."

"Mrs. Marino. Is that you, Mrs. Marino." The sound was getting closer.

No, it was someone else. Antonio would have said, 'Johanna.' Not 'Is that you, Mrs. Marino?'

"We need your help," the voice said as it drew closer.

Johanna was bewildered. She couldn't move, torn between going toward the voice calling her back toward her cabin and the voice she imagined coming from the sea. Distraught with grief, she scarcely saw the seaman who was approaching her. Then she heard a baby cry.

"My baby, my baby," she pleaded.

"No," said the seaman. "This baby was born last night in steerage. His mother didn't make it. Neither will the baby if he doesn't have a wet nurse. Considering your loss I hate asking you, but you're the baby's only chance. Will you nurse him?"

Johanna took a deep breath and drew back the heavy cloak that covered the baby. Her heart almost stopped.

"Yes, yes," Johanna cried. "What is his name?"

"Call him what you like. His mother never revived."

He helped Johanna return to her cabin with the bundled

baby, promising to return when he could.

"The doctor, when is he coming?"

"He sent me to you. He had been attending the mother and was quite upset that the birth did not bode well for her. He needs to sleep tonight as he has a high fever. The captain has ordered him to stay in his cabin for awhile and rest. I'll come back tomorrow if the doc asks me to do so."

Johanna never saw the doctor again. He was among the forty-three passengers and crew who died aboard the ship of the measles. The little baby boy that the seaman brought to Johanna was robust and healthy. He cheered Johanna though she still mourned little Maria and Antonio. The baby suckled hungrily, and blew little bubbles at Johanna. She found herself smiling and cooing to the child.

The baby loved Johanna's long chestnut locks which she hadn't bothered to put into a bun since confined to the cabin. He would grasp a few hairs and twist them until they became tangled. Johanna laughed as she brushed out the tangles - the first interest she had shown in her hair or appearance since Antonio became ill.

"You're a little spit-fire aren't you? I wonder what they'll call you."

Johanna suddenly realized the baby wasn't hers. Not hers to name and certainly not hers to keep.

The baby thrived under Johanna's loving care. As the days went by, she was drawn to the cloak, which she was using as a make-shift mattress stuffed in a drawer. The baby boy had been wrapped in it when brought to her. Remembering the girl she had seen the first day out and her lovely smile when she caught the orange, Johanna thought. She had been wearing this cloak. Johanna was certain of it. Poor thing! Now she was buried at sea with Maria and Antonio and numerous others.

Lifting the cloak to her face, she said a silent prayer for the lovely girl.

Wait, what's this, Johanna thought, feeling a strange

JOHANNA

lump in the cloak. Exploring the cloak, she found a coin in the lining. Pulling out the coin she examined it, then looked carefully, seam by seam. Leaving the rest of the coins, Johanna estimated the number.

Why was this girl in steerage when she had all this money? Johanna pondered. Well, maybe the coins are not worth much. They must be Greek coins or perhaps Turkish. Johanna did not know the value of the one she held in her hands.

As she examined the cloak carefully, she discovered the letters - letters from a lover, and other items.

Johanna spent the next hour examining the packet of letters. To some extent she felt ashamed reading someone else's mail, some of it quite intimate. Some contained valuable information, however, especially one. It read as follows:

Dear Cassandra,

It is with great sadness that I have asked this lad to find you. I only hope there's a God or gods who will help him do so. It will take many days.

By the time he arrives I will have succumbed to my wounds. As I die, it is with joy for knowing you and for sharing the short time we had together. My regret is that I'll never see our child.

As you know, my family is mostly deceased. There is no one to help you other than my older brother in New York. His address is on the back of this paper. I trust this boy, Erjon, completely. He has been with us since before I met you and has been stalwart in his help. I know that if at all possible the lad will bring you the money. I trust it will help you get to the 'promised land' where our son or daughter will thrive. I'm glad you still have my cloak. When it is cold at sea, wrap in it and pretend it is my arms around you, as that is where they wish to be.

My love, it is taking all of my strength to write this to you. You're my heart - my soul. I fear for the wrath of your family when they learn about our child. Your ingenious ways to meet me in secrecy give me courage that you can find a way to reach my brother before our baby breathes air on its own.

Our destiny is to be together again someday - perhaps in another age when war is past and men have learned to live in peace and love.

Til then, my love, farewell,
Your Niccolò

Johanna read this letter for the third time. Who would know if I kept the baby?

The ship's doctor of course. It was not to be.

Fascinated that she now knew the full name of the father and the first name of the girl who died, she realized that the babe was truly an orphan. Probably his uncle would be named the guardian. When the doctor came back, she would have to tell him about the letter. It would only be right.

Johanna grew closer to the babe each day. She dreaded the doctor's return. After several days she began to hope he had forgotten her and the boy. Yes, only he would know if she kept the baby? After all, it would be months before the baby would not need her milk. And what a precious child he was, a child of love. The story was there in the letters from the babe's father. The baby's parents had shared the kind of passionate love that few couples ever experience.

JOHANNA

CHAPTER ELEVEN
A PATH SO STEEP
Somewhere In Albania

"These Indian ponies are remarkable," observed the tall uniformed man. "I never imagined terrains this treacherous or I would not have volunteered for this journey."

"They are Spiti ponies; tolerant of cold and short rations. It is said they can smell glaciers and take a safe path away from them," responded the guide.

"I wouldn't exactly call these paths. It's as if the ponies steer their way up, edging along the side of cliffs and around jagged rocks that barely have space between them for the sleds carrying the wounded."

"Makes my job as a guide easier. How are the patients?"

"Most are sleeping at least. Three have fevers too high for a man. I don't see how they can live to get up to the top."

The guide grimaced. "These Albanians are made of strong stuff. They seem to understand we are taking them to a famous healer. They don't speak much do they?"

"Only the one. He keeps calling for Cassandra. He is delirious!" said the soldier.

"Maybe it is a war cry the way he shouts. But I'll bet it is a woman; he wears a woman's ring around his neck. It looks expensive."

"I'm surprised he still has it. Those ruffian kids, they were picking the fighters clean."

"Must've been his odor. His wound smells so rancid they probably didn't get close."

"Who is this famous physician we are seeking," asked

the soldier.

"He was captured and tortured and refuses to go anywhere but this monastery now. He lived somewhere in Asia - skilled in both Western and Eastern medicine. Some of the older physicians laughed at his methods. He uses herbs; no bleeding. Things they relied on like leeches he wouldn't touch. When he was captured he cured a dying leader and they called him a witch doctor.

"The captors wanted to burn him or to cut off his fingers. The leader he had healed would not let them kill him. He said 'a life for a life. You may torture him but only on one part of his body. Make sure the torture is not so severe that he dies from it.'

"'His hand then; fingers on his right hand. He will forever regret a hand with no fingers.'

"'My fingers are not me,' the physician exclaimed. 'Go ahead; cut them off. I still have my face. My face is me!'

"This amused the captors. They began just beneath his ears while the doctor protested loudly. The physician endured the torture which greatly disfigured him. However he kept his fingers which were vital for a surgeon. He remains sharp eyed with skilled hands."

"Let's hope we get there soon with no more deaths. Pray that your physician is still around," replied the soldier.

JOHANNA

CHAPTER TWELVE
LAND OF THE FREE
New York City
April 1912

"Land ahoy," came the shout from the crow's nest.

Johanna rushed to the deck. Standing there she held the baby up to watch as slowly the Statue of Liberty grew from a tiny speck to the lady herself.

For Johanna it was a time of intense and conflicting feelings - relief the ship had finally arrived and anxiety about the boy. Hurriedly, Johanna returned to her cabin. She had no papers for the boy - no birth certificate. She feared they would take him from her!

A seaman appeared to give her information about what to expect on arrival. He would be back to help her with her things in the cabin. Her trunks would be sent by courier and should arrive within two or three days. If she could give him an address now it would greatly expedite her departure from the ship.

"I should speak to the ship's doctor," she said.

"Unfortunately, he fell victim to this red rash disease," was the reply. "He left us three days ago. Where would you like your trunks delivered. Or it a wagon is waiting I can call one of the seamen to help you."

I will take him to his uncle myself, she decided quickly. The address is there with the letters. With Antonio gone I have no other plan anyway.

Johanna wasted no time giving the seaman the address

of Arian Zantos, the brother of the babe's father.
Palming one of the small coins she had taken earlier from the lining of the cloak, Johanna handed it to the seaman.

"How much will you need to send the trunks? There are two more in the storage area; one quite heavy."

The seaman smiled broadly.

"This is most generous. I can send change with the trunks."

"No, keep it. You have been most helpful during this dreadful trip. I'll take care of the final person delivering the trunks."

Taking the papers the doctor had signed for her unfortunate baby girl, she quickly scribbled a few words, checking M to indicate a male baby.

"This will have to be enough to get us through Immigration," Johanna said to the sleeping baby.

As the seaman hinted, exiting the ship went quickly from that point. She had read that physicians came from the city to do the on-ship physicals of the passengers but the young woman noticed no such procedure. It must be for steerage only, she thought, relieved that she had one less hurdle to manage without questions regarding the baby. Johanna's papers showed a mother and a baby. Johanna did not show them the scrawled death certificate of her little daughter. Why get into a controversy over whether the baby belonged in steerage and would have to go to Ellis Island? By the time this was all resolved, they could be separated. Worse still, the baby could die of hunger. That would not be! Johanna gratefully left the ship with the child in her arms, quickly boarding the transport that took most of the first class passengers to a pier on the mainland.

Johanna took a deep breath when the small boat landed. Having haunted the library near their Italian villa to learn about immigration policies and papers and monies needed

JOHANNA

on arrival in the land of freedom, she was worried.

Stepping away from the transports and onto solid land thus was a great relief to Johanna. She took a deep breath of free if not quite fresh air. The fishy rotten smell of the docks were preferable to the smell of fear that she could lose this baby.

Johanna looked around for some kind of transport when a gentleman noticed and hailed a Hanson cab. It delighted Johanna to see the horse approach pulling the cute little two-person buggy so familiar to her on the London streets. She knew once situated she would have privacy to feed the baby, who certainly was smacking his little lips already. The Hanson cabs had a wooden partition between the driver and passengers to protect the latter from slush, stone, rain and wind, while the driver faced the elements perched above the horse and the partition.

"Take me to the best hotel you know with room service," she told the driver.

She was in no mood to give up the freedom and independence she felt among all the activity in this bustling city. Buildings were going up everywhere and the streets were filled with vendors, construction gangs and shoppers. The excitement - the life - so vibrant in the city - boded hope. Hungry and tired, Johanna would not go to find Arian today. It was almost night anyway and he lived in a place called the Bronx. She needed to find a map, but most of all she needed sleep. Or was food her greatest motivation? She couldn't remember if they had brought breakfast to her with all the excitement of landing.

After a luxurious night with dinner in her room and a bath for a queen, Johanna realized how grubby her clothes had become. From the time she boarded the Matilda, she had worn the same two outfits day after day. The others were packed in the stored trunks.

She threw the outfit away that was hopelessly soiled between the birth of her daughter and all of Antonio's excretions during his illness. Not giving it a second thought she kept the room for another night and went shopping in downtown Manhattan - first stop a sling to carry the baby; then clothes for him and herself.

Knowing she should be in mourning, Johanna chose four outfits in black. Then, unable to resist the soft blues and vibrant greens among the newest ankle-length styles, she added two dresses and a white and a grey blouse to soften the two black pleated skirts that comprised the lower portions of two of the widows' attire.

Thoroughly cheered by her lovely choices she returned to her room to feed the baby, ordering oysters and a steak for herself. She tried on her new outfits, washed her hair, and sorted the baby clothes, realizing as she did so that this baby had almost outgrown the size she had chosen. They would just have to go back to the shop with the best baby clothes. Wasn't it the one with the most interesting hat she had seen in a window and regretted that her arms could carry nothing more?

Baby and all Johanna returned to the streets. She exchanged the baby things for larger sizes and purchased another even larger sized wardrobe for him. She wanted to make sure he had something from her, even if she had to leave him.

A hawker selling newspapers drew Johanna's attention.

"Get your paper here. Read all about it," he shouted. "The unthinkable has happened. The Unsinkable is underwater. The great Titanic is gone. The Titanic sank. Read all about it."

It can't be, Johanna thought. It was built a special way. The brochure said it couldn't sink!

What if ....?

Suddenly chill bumps covered her body. She fumbled in a pocket for change and waved to the paper vendor, completely forgetting the hat.

JOHANNA

Back at the hotel when the baby fell asleep, Johanna read every word written in the paper about the ill-fated ship.
"What a horrible experience. The old Matilda at least got most of us here," she whispered to the baby.

Woken in the middle of the night by the hungry child the woman felt a deep sense of urgency. Her mind was sharp and her intent was clear. As she nursed the baby she talked to him telling him what she thought they must do.
"We were meant to come here - you and I. If I keep you one more day, I'll never be able to give you to your uncle, but I must do it. My choice of ships was wrong. It will turn out just as wrong if I pretend you are my child and the child of Antonio."
This realization spurred her to act. She carefully packed her new purchases in her already crowded trunk and valise. Taking the baby in his sling and her valise in the hand not supporting the child she walked down the stairs to the lobby, noticing for the first time the lovely carpet covering the wide, well-lit stairway. She felt a tingling all up and down her spine as she watched herself descend the steps in the huge mirrors that adorned the walls to either side. She saw a woman grown - no longer the teen who had first boarded the Matilda with misgivings. She was wearing the cloak of the child's birth mother draped over her shoulders. No opera cape had ever draped so beautifully. Johanna saw for the first time the woman she had come to be: a woman full grown walking with grace and purpose.

The night clerk cautioned Johanna that the midnight hour was approaching. She should at least allow him to arrange for a motor car with a trusted driver, since she was determined to go to the Bronx in spite of the hour.
"It will take less than half an hour to call the limousine service we use and meanwhile I'll have someone get the trunk and extra parcels from your room. Since you have paid for the entire night, the club room will serve you wine

or sherry while you wait, along with an appetizer of your choice."

The club room was anything but relaxing as it was filled with conversations about the Titanic. It seemed as if every person there knew someone coming to New York on the tragic vessel. The baby stretched and looked wide-eyed directly at Johanna as she sipped her first taste of sherry.

"Now?" She asked the baby. "Can I do it now?"

JOHANNA

CHAPTER THIRTEEN
MY BROTHER'S KEEPER
The Bronx, New York

It was a rare occasion when Arian Zantos had visitors except for Joule, his former colleague as a Freedom Fighter and now his landlord.

Tonight he had two strangers arrive; one more of a surprise than the other.

Joule brought both.

The first had no name that he shared. Both Albanians knew he had been sent by the Godfather of one of the Syrian Mafia's branches that had claimed rights in the New World.

"I'm afraid I have bad news," the visitor said. "A few nights ago the operative who was stealing machine guns from a German arsenal was shot in the act. The only good thing - he was dead as he fell, so there was no inquisition about where he was taking the guns."

"That is a grave concern," Arian answered. Arian headed up the supply ring that operated out of New York City, while Joule took charge of soliciting money.

"They are heavily guarding the arsenal now, hoping we will send someone else they can capture alive. Your recruitment tactics are to be admired. The man who was shot had no family; therefore no one to question."

The Sicilian smiled.

"We are clean but our Don discourages use of that site again for quite a while."

"That is good to hear," Arian answered. "No Don wants the iron hand of the Kaiser interfering with his business."

"Do not fear. My Don will never allow that. He is no longer willing to help the Albanian cause, however. Personally, I wish you well, but it is the Don's call to make."

"Do you have any news of my brother?"

"Only that he was most probably the 'migrant worker' that was sent under cover to an area in Greece where the numbers of arrival 'merchandise' was consistently higher than the numbers of items arriving at the next safe haven. He found the thief that was intercepting your shipments. Not only that, he found where these stolen items were stored and worked with his team to move in equipment to retrieve them. That raid was led by the 'man who looks like a boy.'

"This boy-man has no name that anyone knows. Your brother was his closest companion. This man that passes as a boy informed us that your brother returned to Albania to resettle orphans after contacting his team and asking the boy-man to lead the retrieval effort.

"If your brother was the undercover agent involved he spent the Summer near the Pindus Mountains. Returning to his home territory to honor a commitment he had made to assist in the orphan resettlement, he ended up in a highly contested combat area. Your brother was wounded badly, fatally it was believed. The boy-man was sent away to convey your brother's dying wishes by none other than the dying man himself.

"That is the bad part of the news. The good is some of a group who were left to care for themselves were discovered. They are hoping to send these men up the mountain to the healer that lives there with the monks. No one knows the identity of the men or which have died and which might be helped by the remote physician."

Arian Zantos was much disturbed by this news. Worried about his brother, he tossed and stretched. Finally he was sleeping soundly when he was awakened once again by pounding on the door.

"Wake up! Wake up!" his landlord shouted. "There's a

JOHANNA

woman here to see you. You know the rules here - no women, but this one has a baby and insists on talking to you."

Arian pulled on his pants under his nightshirt and stumbled to the door. The woman who stood meekly behind his landlord looked exhausted. This had to be the woman who had written him, his brother's lover.

Johanna held out the baby. As soon as Arian took the boy, she collapsed on the floor. The building superintendent, Joule, grimaced.

"I'm going to have to make an exception I see. She can stay the night but tomorrow she has to go. Some of the other fellows staying here will see her and think they can turn this place into a henhouse."

"Help me get her to the bed," Arian pleaded. "Or take the baby and I will carry her. This is my brother's baby and if her letter to me was right, the baby's fatherless. My brother died fighting Turks."

"It's alright, little one," Joule took the baby. "We'll do right by you. Your father was a hero then!"

The building where Arian lived was one of a number in a section of the Bronx in which numerous Albanian immigrants had settled. Arian himself had been a Freedom Fighter and was considered a hero by his comrades in the city. He had learned from various sources that a bounty had been placed on his head. This information came as no surprise since Arian had led many successful raids on properties owned by the Pashas. He was forced to choose between fleeing Albania and facing a painful death. Arian chose a new life in the New World where he could most likely afford to send money to support his cause.

The baby was settled in a bed made from a dresser drawer and his mother's cloak. Joule changed and bathed the little one, a task Arian had never before observed.

Johanna tossed restlessly. She woke and began to

explain her reasons for coming.

"Sleep, lady," Arian told her. "We'll talk tomorrow."

"Yes, soon I will sleep," Johanna replied. "I must feed the baby first."

Before Arian made a bed for himself on the floor, he thumbed through personal papers until he found the letter he sought.

Dear Mr. Zantos,

I hope this letter finds you in good health. It is with great sadness that I must inform you of the recent demise of your brother, Niccolò.

Niccolò fought bravely in the struggle for a free and independent Albania. He is survived by a tiny babe yet unborn.

I am the fortunate woman who will bear Niccolò's son, for I am sure it is a son. We were to travel together to America to make a new life. Now I must find my way there alone and I desperately need your help upon arrival. Niccolò believed that without a sponsor they might send us back to Greece.

I am willing to nurse the child and make him yours if you so require. Certainly I am willing to find work. I sew beautifully. I hope we can find a way to share your home as this was Niccolò's desire and I feel the far best option for your nephew.

Please respond to my Aunt's address, which I will indicate below.
Ever in your debt,
Cassandra Marie Vladimar Zantos

JOHANNA

CHAPTER FOURTEEN
EQUAL FOOTING

Arian lived in one room on a lower floor of the tenement, sharing the toilet with all others on his floor. His work in a nearby laundry would have enabled him to afford a two or three-bedroom apartment, but he preferred to save all he could and live humbly. Part of his salary he sent to the Albanian Patriots.

Arian hated his job. His dream was to own a restaurant - or at least to be a Head Cook in a decent restaurant. He particularly wanted to specialize in Mediterranean food. By living frugally he hoped to lease or own a restaurant in a few years.

The next morning Joule arrived early with coffee, milk and apples.

"All I can find is a loft nearby. It has been for rent for two months. It is furnished and vacant. The landlord is one of us and has agreed that the woman and babe can stay there for a week. You'll have to pay for the water and gas and if she stays longer there will be rent. Are you going with them?"

"No, she can go alone or find another place when she gets work. I'll keep the baby here."

"Don't be absurd! Where will you get a wet nurse? This isn't a mountain village back home! It will be months before the baby can eat table food."

Arian was abashed. He had not thought of that.

"Well then, can you sublet this? I certainly can't pay for two places and your darn rules say I can't keep her here."

"Manny on the floor above has been asking for a room for his cousin. Maybe he'll take it. I'll help you move your things when you get back from work. Meanwhile, let's take them over. You won't have her on your hands for long. From what I saw last night, she is marriageable material. Greek is she?"

"She doesn't look Greek to me. She sounds English. I wonder if she is the one who wrote or someone employed to bring the baby here. Let's wake her and get her settled. I don't want to be late for work."

Thus, Johanna, armed with the babe, the cloak that had been the lovely woman's in steerage and all her new purchases, was directed to follow the strangers. As they were exiting the building, a wagon arrived bringing her trunks and luggage. She slipped a coin from her pocket to give the wagon driver, but Joule interceded, giving the driver three copper colored American coins. Joule and Arian lifted the trunks from the wagon, then called a boy over to take the bags. They walked two blocks carrying the trunks as if they were feathers.

The landlord of the new building was thin and bald, but easily assisted with the trunks. Up a thousand stairs went the party - trunks, bags, men, boy, baby and Johanna. When the landlord opened the door, Johanna gasped with surprise. A large window covered much of the ceiling of the spacious room in which she found herself. Sun was streaming through the window, brilliantly lighting the area. Johanna thought the room was smiling at her and she smiled back.

The room was painted blue, the shade of a robin's egg, just a little darker than the sky outside. At one end was a black wood stove that the landlord had lit earlier. On one side of the stove was a rag rug and a small baby's bed complete with a mattress and coverlet.

To the other side of the stove, a tall cabinet stood next to an open shelf. A metal rack hung from the ceiling with a couple of pots dangling from it. A round wooden table with four sturdy chairs sat in front of the cabinet.

The far side of the room contained a desk - it looked very old, its roll top halfway down and a loose drawer slightly opened and ill-fitting. The remaining object amazed Johanna. She drew in her breath. A piano was displayed proudly in a corner of the room! A real piano!

"The same couple lived here for twenty years," the landlord was saying. "They made what they called improvements, like the skylight. I almost boarded it up - no one wants an apartment with a window that can't be opened, closed, or covered! I say it just takes some time getting use to it. When the weather is clear the stars shine like ice - the cold kind not the kind all women love. The bedrooms are in the back through the door there. One is very small."

The door led into a hall. On one side was a gigantic bedroom fully furnished with a double wide bed. Across the hall was a small room with a treadle sewing machine.

"They paid to put in this bathroom," the landlord said, opening another door. "It is something of an extravagance. It was the best that money could buy. It took up most of the second bedroom, however." Johanna marveled at the bath. She turned on the water and found it hot. The large tub had claw feet. A toilet with a pull string flush mechanism complemented the basin which also had running water. Cabinets and mirrors were ample and beautifully arranged.

"I'll take the small room," Arian said. "You and the baby can have the other. When he wakes up at night, you might like the space to walk around. If he's fussing, you won't want to change from your nightclothes. Some nights I work extra and come home late. I can heat something to eat in the other room and not bother you. I'll need a bed though. Can we move this sewing stuff into your room or store it?"

"Please, I can use it. There's plenty of room. The baby and I can even take the small room."

"Boy," Arian demanded, "Move these boxes into the big

room. She'll show you where. I'm off to work."

Left alone with the boy and baby, Johanna had him rock the little one while she unpacked her things. The boy was quite willing to do her bidding. She had him rearrange the large bedroom, moving one of the chests from there into the small bedroom for Arian. They moved the baby's bed and sewing equipment into the large bedroom and used the bathtub to wash the sheets from the large bed that was now Johanna's. The boy was fascinated by the tub, so she ran him a bath, leaving him to soak while she fed the baby.

Unable to find even a broken cup in either the cupboard or large cabinet she grabbed her coat and called the boy, clean now except for his grubby clothes.

"I must buy cups and food. Can you show me where?" Johanna asked him.

Food sounded great to the boy. He brought Johanna quickly to a street vendor selling hot dogs. Johanna laughed and bought one for each of them. Rounding a corner, he pointed to a second hand store.

"The tinker sells cups there," he said.

"Get out of here, Zack!" the tinker shouted as the boy darted in ahead of Johanna.

"He is with me," Johanna said. "I have purchases to make and I need help carrying them."

"Sorry," said the man. "Zack can be a pest, but I'm glad he is helping you. You may regret it though. He has a bottomless well for a stomach!"

"Here Zack," Johanna laughed. "You sit over here and hold the baby while I look around."

Johanna paid for her purchases. She and the boy carried what they could.

"I'll have the rest delivered within the hour," the storekeeper promised. "You have the iron bedstead and carved wooden wardrobe with mirror along with the box of dishes, a black skillet and a sturdy rocking chair. Is that all or do you want to look around some more?"

JOHANNA

"The mattress for the small bed," Johanna replied.

"That has to come from the warehouse. I'll send word right away and you should have it by nightfall," the tinker scratched his chin.

One more stop assured delivery of some basic groceries including tins of vegetables, sardines and salmon, as well as coffee, tea, herbs, fresh eggs and a lamb roast.

When Arian arrived that evening with a wooden crate filled with his belongings, he was astounded. The table was set with a blue check cloth and white dishes that were painted in blue with mountain scenes. A hearty soup filled the loft with aromas reminiscent of his mother's kitchen in Albania. Johanna was just taking fresh bread from the oven.

Joule arrived just behind Arian with a second crate.

"Praise Allah," he exclaimed. "I told you she would be marriage material. She won't last until the baby can eat."

"I just buried one husband at sea," Johanna blushed. "I have no intention of taking another."

"At sea? Then Niccolò lived after all?" Arian asked.

"Oh, no - I'm not Niccolò's wife. She died in childbirth on the ship. My baby girl and my husband also died on board and they brought me this baby to nurse. Your address was in her things and, well, here I am and here I'll stay. Hopefully you and the baby will stay here too, but for now let's eat while the soup is hot. Joule, I set a place for you."

The boy was the first to take a seat.

"You, boy - what are you still doing here?" Joule asked roughly.

"He has been helping me all day - showing me the shops, cleaning, changing the baby, moving furniture - we have worked up an appetite, haven't we, Zack?"

The boy grinned. Shortly after eating he disappeared. So did the second loaf of bread, Johanna noticed.

Johanna and Arian put off serious conversations until his next day off. He was working extra hours, peeved that he needed to do so to pay for her purchases. Early morning on his day off he went to the secondhand store to see how much he owed. When told Johanna had paid for everything, he was appalled - that was not how it should be. The woman had shamed him. Shamed him, yet he also felt relieved - even delighted. Arian didn't know how to feel. What kind of woman was she? Meat pies and apple cakes filled his stomach, and the baby filled a place in his heart close to the way he had felt when Niccolò was a tot.

The grocer, too, said there was no outstanding debt. The English woman paid in advance of delivery actually and he was giving her a discount for the cash.

"With so many families on the tab, this is a blessing. Where did you find her?"

"She is a distant relative," Arian lied. "My brother died in our native country, Albania, and she was traveling here with my brother's wife. Unfortunately, when my nephew was born, the wife and my brother were united in death."

"It is your duty then to take her in. Well, she will be courting soon unless you put a claim on her. You could certainly do worse."

"She is English. I am Muslim," Arian said. "But don't send suitors anytime soon. She lost her husband and the child she bore on the ship and she is in mourning yet."

A noise caught their attention. The grocer moved quickly, grabbing a boy by the ear.

"I gave you fruit yesterday! Would you steal from me today?"

"I was only taking the bruised apple," the boy pleaded.

Arian interrupted. "You left our loft in a hurry the other day, Boy. What did she call you? Zack? I had a coin for you. Will you stop by later?"

The grocer bopped Zack on the ear, but then handed him the apple after all.

Back at the loft Arian found Johanna putting down the baby. The door to her room was open and he clearly saw the tenderness with which she handled the child.

When she turned toward him, he motioned for her to come.

"No work today?" she asked, following him to the table.

"They make us take off one day in every ten. It's time we talked. I went to the grocer and the tinker. They said you had paid them already. This cannot be. You're under my care. I pay the bills."

"If you took a wife would you not take her dowry? My husband certainly did. He considered every penny of my trust to belong to him on the day it arrived. Had it not been prearranged that I would receive it in monthly installments, I do believe it would be gone by now."

"You have a monthly allowance? Then why do you need me? Why come here at all? You could have lived on your own and never told me that the baby arrived safely."

"Then what kind of woman would I be? Not fit for mothering a child, that's for sure. Besides, the babe's mother is in heaven watching over my angel baby. She was bringing Nicki here to you. I cannot break faith with her. A part of me did wish that you would turn us away. More of me feared that you would. After the harrowing trip - the storms and the deaths, I cannot bring myself to get right back on a ship even though I know I have a home and family in England. A woman alone in this city would be at risk daily. I felt danger at every corner as I searched for this neighborhood."

"That is true. Indeed, if you're going to do the shopping and such we might get the boy, Zack, to accompany you. When you go out, you take the baby of necessity. You would be safer with someone streetwise like the lad."

"If I could find him that would be ideal. Do you know where he lives?"

"Does anyone? Every neighborhood has children. Street kids who don't live anywhere. They wander around, stealing food, trying to stay out of one another's territory while gradually enlarging their own."

"Where do they come from? They must have parents."

"Some say from the brothels. The women there are said to keep and nourish them as babies and youngsters. Then they either toss them out on their own or use them in ways a lady never dreams possible - those that are thrown out are the lucky ones, believe it! Some are runaways from the church orphanages. Some are from families who cannot feed them or are cruel. Some seem to sprout up from thin air like a weed."

"That is so horrid. So you think Zack has no home?"

"The cousin taking my room never showed up, so I have to pay for it. You can offer it to the boy at least through the fall and winter. In return he is to check with you every day I work and go with you if you want to explore - especially if you wander outside this neighborhood.

"Now back to the money! You have expensive tastes but I have to admit we needed what you purchased that first day. Furthermore, you haven't continued this spending except for food. If you do any more shopping like the first day, people will think I'm stealing money. If they find out that you have an income, many will try to force a marriage either by guile or by giving you a child."

"What do you suggest? I know! Your coins!" shouted Johanna. "I had forgotten to mention it. I don't really know if it's much. I found the coins in Cassandra's things. She was sent the money by the messenger who brought her the news of Niccolò's death. I read it in her letters!

"It doesn't matter if it isn't much, does it? We can still call it an inheritance and for all anyone knows it could be a small fortune. I think the coins are Greek - or maybe Turkish. Niccolò found a riderless horse with a bed roll and other belongings. I think that is how he got at least some of the coins. Wait. I'll get them for you."

Arian was stunned. Had Nic sent him bounty from a slain Turk?

"Niccolò sent this to Cassandra to help her find you. The baby should have been born here in this country, but the

JOHANNA

storm threw us off course and the voyage took forever," Johanna was saying, her voice drifting away as she saw Arian's face. She had meant to say there were more coins that she could ease out of the cloak, but she stood frozen instead as Arian found his voice.

"These were from Nic? And you brought them to me? Why, we could buy this building with them! Johanna, we will split them. You take half!"

"Oh, let's buy the building instead - for you and little Nicki and for me as long as possible. You can have the building and I can live in this beautiful loft and help Zack a little. I don't want the coins. I want the companionship and security. I was greatly drawn to the girl who conceived this baby. She was so beautiful and so young. Please take the coins. I feel that she saved them just for you and for her baby's future."

And so it was that Arian and Johanna became landlords and made improvements in the apartments below the loft. He found a person to sublet his old room and installed Zack in a studio apartment on a lower floor of their building. He encouraged Johanna to furnish it, but not elaborately.

She made one more significant purchase - sheet music - and tuned the piano herself.

Arian refused extra hours at the laundry so he could take care of issues in the tenement. It had its share of leaky faucets, broken windows and peeling paint. Zack was a quick learner and able assistant in this regard.

Every ten days, on Arian's day off, the four went on an adventure - to museums in Manhattan, an amusement park on Coney Island, zoos in the Bronx and Central Park. Usually they took a bus. When little Nicki outgrew his sling, Johanna fashioned a backpack out of strong twill fabric. The baby could then be strapped in and carried easily by any of the adults. Much to Nicki's delight this gave him a bird's eye view as they walked along.

From time to time Johanna thought of the coins sewn in

the lining of Cassandra's cloak. She had meant to give them all to Ari. The longer she waited the worse it seemed to her to have held them back. Antonio would have spent them foolishly. Arian had spent most of the ones given him, but not foolishly. Buying the building and making improvements was an investment - something tangible. Still if an emergency occurred - an accident to Ari or an illness contracted by one of them or the baby - it might be hard to liquidate the building immediately. She rationalized that the coins she kept back would be available for emergencies. However, she had her allowance for emergencies. The coins belonged to Ari; she would give them to him soon.

JOHANNA

CHAPTER FIFTEEN
SUMMER IN NEW YORK CITY
1912

Many of the millions of immigrants thought of America as the 'Promised Land' where they would find riches and success. Some were brought as indentured servants with dreams of a life of freedom once they had paid for their passage by their labor. Some came because they were persecuted in their native land due to their beliefs. Each person had a story - a hope - a need to make the trip. For Johanna the purposes of her journey changed en route due to the unforseen travails aboard the ship. They also changed for many of the travelers. Still, they dreamed! So long as there is a dream, the human spirit can triumph.

Summer in New York City is an outdoor time. The parks attract the rich and poor, musicians and street peddlers, hot dog vendors and pretzel sellers. The Bronx Zoo was a favorite of Johanna's. Nicki could contentedly watch the monkeys for hours. One advantage was the Zoo's proximity - no sizzling hot subways to contend with.

Zack blossomed under Johanna's care. He was no longer a grubby beggar but rather a handsome preteen, tall and agile with a smile for everyone. His nature had always been friendly, but now he felt that fortune smiled on him and he emanated happiness.

Keeping Johanna and Nicki safe was his primary purpose in life, but that included having fun with them. His favorite outing was to Coney Island and his favorite food was hot dogs - especially those on Coney Island. Johanna treated

Zack like a younger brother who had many needs. While he knew the value of every coin minted in the USA he couldn't read or write his name. Johanna began to teach him to read street signs and store names. She had tried books first but Zack almost seemed allergic to sitting down and looking at an open book.

"We couldn't have books or newspapers where I first lived," he explained. "Those caught with one were punished."

Johanna questioned Zack further about his earlier living arrangements.

He turned morose and shrugging his shoulders he faintly whispered.

"Long time ago. I don't talk about it."

Arian had a restless summer. He thought of Johanna as a friend and business partner. Or so he told himself. It had been months since he had been with a woman. If Johanna had been less of a beauty, Arian might've been able to handle things better. As it was, no other woman could compare. He asked a friendly woman to go out and canceled at the last moment. He went to a brothel - which he had never preferred. After paying he left, unable to get past the woman's brazenness and nudity.

By mid-July Arian was finding excuses to come home late. He took extra hours again in the laundry, saving building maintenance for his days off and sending Johanna, Nicki and Zack on outings without him though this pained him.

By August he had formed a habit of stopping at a bar on the way home. One beer became a couple, then a couple of beers soon became several.

Better she is in bed and sleeping before you come back! Arian chided himself. If she suspected what he was dreaming she would leave them for London immediately. Perhaps she is already preparing to go! He knew she had exchanged letters with family back in England. Is it only

JOHANNA

family or does she have a handsome suitor?

    Arian was nearly mad for wanting Johanna. He knew a lady of independent means such as she would want intimacy only in her marriage bed. Allah had sent him a trial by fire and he knew he was handling it badly. The temptation was overpowering; he coveted a Christian no less!
    No, I do not just covet her body. I fear I love her, Arian silently admitted. He loved little Nicki also, and the two of them seemed to go together.
    How would either of us get by without her? he wondered.
    She was laughter. She was warmth. She was softness to be held and honored. She was joy and life and lust - yes, lust. With such recurrent thoughts as these, each night Arian drifted off into dreamland. There he found her in bed with him of her own free will. In sweet, mellow dreams she lay on the crook of his arm and vowed that she would never leave them. In passionate, vivid dreams she opened her body to him and gave all that he gave in the way a man and a woman love.

    Johanna on the other hand was happy as a lark. She had accepted her first week in New York that she was attracted to Arian physically as well as every other way. To her, the only practical outcome was that they would eventually become man and wife. If not formally as she hoped, then as common law spouses. How else could they both raise Nicki?
    If Arian had been unattractive she would have overlooked that. If Arian had been totally out of shape and/or a bully, she would have thought him no worse than Antonio. Antonio behind his charming exterior was no man that any woman could desire. Arian, though! This man was a man any woman would be proud to call her own. She had found her life partner and she wanted to share life with him in every way!

As the summer progressed Johanna was annoyed that Arian was spending so little time with them. She had enjoyed the evenings together, especially when they were alone after Nicki was asleep and she and Arian had long conversations. He liked to hear her play the piano, and it been almost a ritual until he started taking double shifts again. She must give him the other coins, but she couldn't just leave them on the breakfast table. At least she should get the coins out of the seams of Cassandra's cloak.

She would stay awake 'til he came in tonight. She would get up in just a minute to make a strong tea so she could stay awake. She could see him now - coming out of the bathroom after his nightly shower. Arian had rigged a contraption so he could sit in the empty tub and rinse off the day's sweat with a spray nozzle attached to a rubber hose. She had seen him once this past month coming out of the bathroom with a towel wrapped around his waist. Arian had disappeared quickly into his bedroom, water still glistening on his muscular back. She fought the urge to follow him and take the towel away to dry his back. At times she wished she had done just that. Her dream was coming now as she was falling asleep. She felt she was following him. He saw her coming and let the towel fall as he took her in his arms. Oh, happy dreams!

JOHANNA

CHAPTER SIXTEEN
ALBANIAN INDEPENDENCE
November 1912

After years of armed struggle the Albanians claimed success. The Turks agreed to their demands and November 28, 1912 was declared 'Independence Day'. Their struggle was complicated by several factors. In October of 1912 Albanian autonomy seemed assured. This alarmed several bordering countries which had hoped to annex parts of Albania for themselves. Armies from Greece, Serbia and Montenegro advanced into Albanian territories.

Delegates gathered from throughout Albania led by Ismail Qemel. Here they issued the Vlorë Proclamation declaring Albania's independence.

Celebrations were held both in Albania and in all places where Albanians had immigrated. Between twenty and thirty thousand immigrants were in the U.S. alone.

Most had settled in urban areas with high concentrations in NYC and Chicago. Ardent nationalists, many had been Freedom Fighters before fleeing Albania. In 1908 they formed a patriotic organization at first named for the Albanian flag: Flamuri I Shqiperise.

The Pan-Albanian Federation of America grew from this organization and had branches in parts of Pennsylvania and Indiana as well as New York and Illinois.

Arian and Joule had the news of Albanian independence before the U.S. press, through wires from friends back home. Johanna often declared that Arian could be heard all the way to Boston, so elated was he when receiving his telegram. Arian had come home early to repair a leak in a tenant's kitchen sink. Johanna signed for the telegram, wondering what it was about, but leaving it folded since it was to Arian. She decided not to wait for him to come back. After repairing the faucet he might not even stop by their apartment before going for a beer. Putting Nicki in his backpack she climbed down to the third floor, and found Arian just putting away his tools.

"Hi, there, little fellow," Arian enthusiastically greeted Nicki, then looked up at Johanna.

"He is getting pretty heavy for you to carry on these stairs," Arian said with concern.

"A telegram just arrived for you. I thought it might be important."

Arian only took a second after looking at the message to grasp the meaning. After his first booming shout, he bowed his head in thankfulness. Looking again at Nicki he spoke seriously,

"You have a native country, boy! At long last we have our native country back. If only your father had lived to see this glorious day!"

A great bonfire was erected in the neighborhood park; a fearfully great fire in the view of many non-Albanians! Families brought snacks and single men brought beer. Musicians turned out in mass and nationalistic music resounded all night. Johanna danced until she had blisters on both feet. She danced with Arian while Zack watched little Nic. She danced with Joule. She danced with the butcher and with people she had never seen before. Finally, exhausted, she took the baby home, leaving Arian who celebrated for the next three days, only stopping by the apartment for a change of clothes, a quick nap and a shower.

Arian celebrated much more than he would have - best to stay away from Johanna. Dancing with her at the celebration had almost been his undoing. If he ever started to make love with her, he feared he could not stop whatever she said. He had no one to talk to about his desire except Joule. They met monthly at meetings of the Albanian Apartment Owners Association, and often more frequently. Afterwards they usually stopped for a beer and the conversation always came around to Johanna. Joule joked that he wanted to be the next in line if Ari decided not to marry her. He liked to make bets regarding how long it would be before Arian and Johanna slept together. Arian refused to bet. The younger man did not like the joking. It came too close to home.

"Shut up, Joule," he said when reminded that the deadline was only a month away that Joule had predicted would be the night of no return.

"I can never marry Johanna. I serve Allah and she prays to the Christian God."

"Nonsense." Joule protested. "Neither of you is very religious that I've noticed. I would not let that interfere with a marriage to such a woman as Johanna. Probably Allah and the Christian God are one and the same anyway, just called different names."

"You sound like an infidel," Arian observed disgustedly.

High in a remote nook of a steep mountain, candles were lit in a monastery. A monk, Brother Gregory, had just arrived with news of the Proclamation. He cautioned quiet optimism.

"How are our patients? They should know of this also."

Brother Christof shook his head sadly.

"We lost another one to an unexplained fever. We still don't know what all they have been exposed to before coming here. Gerant was getting better, but became delirious in his sleep two nights ago. He passed on yesterday morning."

Brother Gregory crossed himself. "A fine lad he was before his injury. The other three?"

"We are pleased with their progress. Especially Niccolò's. If any of the three have a will to live, it is Niccolò."

"I fear he will never join our order. When he was close to comatose he would utter no words except a woman's name - that of the goddess, Cassandra."

"Hmm," mumbled Brother Gregory. "Perhaps I've met this woman. So you think he might make it?"

"He is finally healing, but it will still be some time before he can walk," a third monk spoke up. "Unless an eagle swoops down to carry him or you find more Spiti's as surefooted as the one's that brought him here, he will be with us for months."

"We were lucky to find such fine beasts," Brother Gregory responded. "Down the mountain was harder for them than up, even without the weight of the wounded. Two had to be shot due to broken legs - unfortunately, both males. The monastery in Kastoria is keeping the females while they look for sires. In early Spring a party will begin a journey to Punjab, India, where the Spiti's are said to be wild. They will not only seek to buy ponies, but try to learn more about their care."

"We will say prayers that they succeed," Brother Christof replied to a chorus of 'Amens' from the others.

"Can we wait until morning to tell the patients' about our Independence? I made sure all three were bedded down over an hour ago and all have been given sleeping powders," a heretofore silent monk wearing a facial mask spoke softly.

"I bow to your judgement. Have you reconsidered my suggestion that you come to a more accessible facility for the wounded? No one has the success that you have."

The Nameless Physician had no doubt in his voice. "When these wounds heal and I succeed in completing my experiments to renew my scared face, I will go down this mountain that I came to with my injuries.

JOHANNA

CHAPTER SEVENTEEN
NOSTALGIA
December 1912

    Christmas had almost arrived and a fresh snowfall had added to the festive streets of the city. Johanna pushed the buggy firmly. It was a recent purchase she thought would be useful, but it certainly was not made for the slush. As she neared the apartment, she saw a young boy on the next street corner hawking Christmas trees.
    She approached, excitedly. The boy had three trees left and she chose the smaller one, paying the boy from the grocery money left in her pocket. She waited as she saw more shoppers approaching. The other trees went quickly and the boy agreed to carry her tree the remaining two blocks for the promise of hot cocoa and fresh baked scones.

    It was such a pleasure to have company for her afternoon tea. Zack had taken a job delivering packages during the holidays. Johanna had taught Zack to ride a bicycle, to the boy's delight. He entertained Johanna with many fun stories about his experiences delivering by bike.
    Arian was almost always at work. On his one day off he was either making repairs and improvements in the apartment building or off somewhere with his cronies.
    The boy was a talker, telling Johanna all about how they celebrated Christmas in his family. Johanna felt suddenly homesick. If only she could go back to England to visit! Alas, Arian would never let her take little Nicki. Further, her experience with ocean travel left her with no desire to ever board a ship again. Two ships contributed to this feeling- the

Matilda where she lost her daughter and husband and the Titanic which had been her choice for transport, a choice luckily vetoed by her husband.

The boy picked up the colored comics from the past Sunday's paper and tore them into strips while Johanna made a flour paste. Soon they had a paper chain to decorate the tree. She found a ribbon she had worn in her hair in younger days. It looked perfect on top of the tree.

When the boy left, Johanna fed Nicki and gave him a bath. Her love for this baby was deep and abiding. He gurgled and grinned at her as she dribbled warm water down his back. If her baby had to die, this was a good exchange. His mother up in the sky taking care of her baby while she took care of Nicki.

Johanna hummed Christmas songs as she cooked. It would be bitter cold tonight when Arian came home. Johanna made his favorite stew, thick with potatoes and onion. However, she took care to spoon some into her bowl before adding a second and third onion.

Later that evening Johanna gave up on seeing Arian when he came home. That is, if he came home that night. She knew he had been asked to work overtime that day but she did not imagine he would be so late. She fed the baby once more, before changing to her pajamas. Yes, she was wearing Antonio's old pajamas as her nightgown was soiled when she delivered the baby alone. She did have one spare gown which she treasured, as she had purchased it for her wedding night. However, the pajamas were comfortable and easy to wash so she found them to be her usual nighttime wear.

Johanna had been asleep, dreaming again of Arian damp from his shower when she heard shouting and stomping. She hurried into the front room.

"Heathen! Heathen!" Arian was shouting. "How dare you bring such an abominable thing into our home?"

JOHANNA

Arian had upended the little tree and was shaking needles all over the room.

"Please Arian, hush. You'll wake the baby," Johanna demanded. "It's just a little tree. Nothing to be upset about. We're in America now! Don't you want the baby to celebrate Christmas the way they do in America?"

Arian could not be hushed. His Islamic heritage coupled with his frustration over his need for Johanna and on top of that skipping supper to work a second shift, left the usually good-natured man angry beyond reason. Grabbing Johanna, he dashed to the nearest chair, throwing her across his lap and making short work of the pajama bottoms which he jerked below her knees.

"I'll teach you to bring heathen symbols into our home!" Arian declared.

He raised his hand and was about to bring his palm down on Johanna's rear; then caught himself. Johanna was not his to correct in any way. If this was a 'home' it was she who had made it so. As suddenly as he had grabbed her, he set her upright.

"I won't apologize for what I was about to do," Arian said. "What you did was disrespectful of my religion and of our home. However, I lost my temper. For that I am ashamed."

Johanna was stunned. The emotions surging through her body were ones she remembered from her early days with Antonio. When Arian lifted her, he had aroused some primaeval need and not just to her. She had felt him grow hard beneath her in the brief moments that he had held her across his lap. Shivers of excitement had rushed through her body and all the way down to her toes.

Johanna fought her desire. The slightest sign from her and surely he would take her to his bed.

Well, isn't that exactly what I want? Johanna chided herself.

She had to say something.

After this night it will be difficult for either of us to live here together without sharing a bed from time to time, Johanna thought. I can't leave the baby and Arian won't part with him. He adores Nicki and feels obligated to his unfortunate brother. Besides, if I am honest with myself, I have wanted this almost since I arrived here.

She went to Arian and took his hand, bringing it to her cheek.

"I meant no disrespect, but I was thoughtless when I purchased the tree," she said. "I should have discussed it with you first. Please, could you just hold me for a moment. I am distraught over the frustration I have caused you."

"If I hold you, I will want more," Arian said, pulling away. "How I have lived with you without touching you so far is nothing less than miraculous. I am human and full of need for you. If I don't leave now and stay away until you are sleeping, something is going to happen from which there is no turning back."

Johanna stood and faced Arian squarely.

"So be it then. It will be my pleasure," she responded, her voice deep and resonant. As she spoke, she unbuttoned her pajama top and let it fall to the floor.

Arian gasped. Taking a deep breath he lifted her in his arms, gently this time, and carried her into his small bedroom. There, he began with soft kisses which caused Johanna to moan so aroused was she.

"My dear little heathen," Arian murmured.

Johanna was experiencing new heights of pleasure far beyond anything she had felt with Antonio. Arian was consuming her, freeing her.

Afterwards they lay side by side without talking, deftly exploring one another with light touches. Aroused again they let their bodies lead them in a dance of passion and tenderness.

Finally they slept until the baby's sweet cries told them morning was beckoning. Arian bid Johanna to stay and brought the baby to her. She fed Nicki there as Arian watched with a look of deep contentment.

JOHANNA

"What will you do when he doesn't need a wet nurse anymore, Johanna? Will you leave us then?" Arian asked, glumly.

"Only if you bid me go," Johanna answered. "And not even then if I can find an excuse to have you change your mind."

"Then from this day onward, as long as we breathe earthly air, I will not touch another woman and I will ask that you likewise stay true only to me," Arian brightened.

Thus it was that Johanna began a new phase of her life - one in which she delighted and thrived.

Arian was always home by suppertime now that things were different between him and Johanna. There was no place he would rather be. He considered it special to play with the baby while Johanna finished preparations for the meal. This day he had come even earlier than usual, taking an hour off at the end of the workday.

"I hoped it would be nap time for Nicki," Arian grinned.

"Not naptime, but some upper grade schools have been advertising a ball game and Zack took Nicki to see what it's all about. They call it football, Zack says, and he thinks a baby not yet a year old will enjoy it."

"You really trust them together, don't you?"

"Yes, and Nicki is just thrilled to go in the stroller with Zack pushing. I was with them until a half hour ago and came back to put the roast in the oven. They should be back in just under an hour."

As she spoke Johanna removed her apron. Then her long skirt.

"Show me how your hose works for bathing while we have some time together. I think it must be fascinating."

"You are the fascinating one. It is a good thing the skylight looks up instead of out If you are going to throw all your clothes off in this room," Arian laughed, lifting the almost nude woman in his strong arms and carrying her to the bathtub, sitting her inside while he disposed of his own clothing.

    Once completely nude, Arian climbed into the tub with Johanna. Arian directed the hose to spray water at Johanna's sensitive body. Johanna laughed in delight as she felt Arian's wet body against hers.

JOHANNA

CHAPTER EIGHTEEN
ENTREPRENEURS
February 1913

As they lingered over their coffee, following the meal. Arian spoke.

"Well, old Mr. Eakins is selling his building across the street. He says this February weather is too much for him. He's going to Florida to live with his son. Somebody will be lucky to get that building. He is selling at the rock bottom price. Much better than the price for which we got this building and that was a fraction of what it is worth. He says he still will make a pretty penny over what he paid originally and his priority is to get away from the cold. His old bones won't take it."

"We should buy it then before someone else snatches it up."

"This time next year we probably could afford it," Arian smiled holding Johanna's hand. "There will be another building then."

"Oh Arian! How could I have forgotten?! There are more coins! I meant to tell you a million times. Cassandra had sewn them into the lining of the cloak. When we talked about it before I had only removed a few. When you saw them and told me how valuable they were, I completely forgot to tell you about the others. I'll get the cloak now and we can ease the coins out of the seams. Maybe there will be more that are worth a lot."

As they looked at the pile of coins they had uncovered, Arian shook his head.

"I don't know whether to be upset because you didn't tell me about these before or overjoyed because we have them! You never fail to amaze me, Johanna, one way or the other!"

Johanna's face was red.

"I know; it is ridiculous that I didn't tell you. The money could have been earning interest in the bank."

"The banks aren't very secure with this talk of all-out war going on in Europe," Arian replied. "The coins were probably safer in the cloak. Maybe you didn't tell me because I was visiting the taverns too often. I couldn't bear to be with you and not touch you. When I think of the time we wasted, I want to burst."

"The important thing now," Johanna observed, "Is do we have enough to buy the building?"

"We'll buy the building and upgrade the apartments one by one as they become empty. We'll put modern kitchens and bathrooms in every apartment and rent them as upscale. It's time we started improving our neighborhood."

The same week that Arian purchased the second building, he shared the letter with Johanna that he had received from Cassandra many months before.

"There is an address for the aunt," Arian said. "I suppose we should write her and tell her about Nicki and about her niece's sad fate.

"I would do so tomorrow," Johanna replied, soberly. "But I cannot write in Greek."

"You help me with the wording, then. I should have written back months ago."

"I have some letters, too, that I found sewn in a pocket of the cloak of riches. I felt hesitant to read them all - but the earliest one led me to you and I thought the second one might be helpful too. I'll get them and we can read them together. They might help with the letter we are writing tomorrow."

JOHANNA

August 17, 1911
Tirana
My dear Cassandra, my wife,
   It is good you did not come with me. The heat is stifling here with no let-up in sight, We had some frightening days when I first arrived. The Serbian army has pushed through Albania, taking Shkoder and Shengjin and is now headed toward Tirana, where I am now.
   I know I promised you I would go to the seaport city of Durres by mid-August to arrange a passage for us before winter. I will still try, but I fear the roads will be blocked due to the fighting.
   How I yearn for you and the summer evenings we spent swimming and learning about one another. I could explore your body and your mind with great joy every evening for the rest of my life. Thankfully, by this time next year we will be settled in America, somewhere near my brother in New York.
   Some of the chaps I knew before I met you have arrived here and tell stories of great unrest and destruction. Enough of that though, my darling. Every night when I lay down to sleep I hold the ring you gave me to honor our union as man and wife, which I keep on a chain around my neck at all times. I stroke its smooth surface and pretend it is your lips that I am stroking.
Good night, my love
Yours forever, Niccolò

   "They were truly in love. I would never have thought that Niccolò would marry one of the Christian faith," Arian looked to Johanna to see her reaction.
   "Perhaps she wasn't a Christian. She was named for one of the Grecian goddesses of old."
   "A pagan, then. She must have been irresistible to a man not yet leaving his teens and on an espionage assignment for a secret organization."
   "This letter is longer. Maybe it will tell us more,"

Johanna observed as she carefully unfolded the thin papers.

August 29, 1911
Elbasan
Dearest

You have my heart, dear Cassie. I have seen so much death and destruction. Thinking of you and our times together - both past and future - are all that keep me whole.

I want our child to grow up in a place of peace. A place with parks and playgrounds not washed with the blood of innocents. What do they say of America? The land of the free - the home of the brave? I think here is the home of many brave souls if bravery involves living day-to-day in spite of the odds that there will be no tomorrow. Certainly though this is no land of the free!

This city is filled with orphaned children. They wear rags even though it has turned quite cold. They beg on the streets. It is hard for me to swallow food sensing their hunger and desperation. I have signed on to help comb the countryside for wandering children who have lost their parents recently. There's a church that helps us reasonably near here. I can't say where lest this letter should fall into the wrong hands. Most of the oldest children already in the city refuse to go. Some are like Wildcats - fearful of everything. Others are so morose that they are wasting away. They are afraid of everyone and everything. Those we find outside the city are perplexed and sad, but not yet hardened by fear and need. There is hope for those if we can get them to the church soon after they lose their parents.

Last night we found a baby in a pile of trash. The poor thing was sleeping - too weak to do anything else. We had no wet nurse of course. We squeezed an orange into its tiny mouth. Then we cleaned her and I carried her in a pouch I made with my jacket. Each step I took I thought of you and our baby nestled inside you. I wanted to rush away with this baby, find you and take all of you to safety!

JOHANNA

I leave for Durres in two weeks. I will do all I can here, but dare not wait longer if we are to get away before the depths of Winter. I hope we can find a steamship well suited to the winter tides. Whatever the ship is like, if we are traveling together it will be a nest of love, a honeymoon worthy of our new start in life.
Love for ever
Niccolò.

"My brother always had the tenderest of hearts, though he was a hearty warrior when need be. Read the next one. I won't sleep now knowing there is more of what he experienced in his last days."

"The next one is short," Johanna observed.

September 2, 1911
Durres
Dearest,
   I must write this hurriedly -fighting goes on all around. The Serbian calvary has arrived and is sweeping the city. I managed to find a horse whose rider was no where to be seen. I am leaving here as soon as possible and coming to you. The horse is a fine one, with a nice saddle and even a bed roll. I will head back toward Elbasan and then South to Greece.
   I do have us on a waiting list for the ship, Pindora, that is due in mid-December, departing just after the New Year. However, if the situation here stays as it is, it will be unsafe to come back. We'll have to consider another port from which to depart, perhaps Vlore or Sarande, which are closer to you at any rate and might get us into Italy or the port near Athens on a feeder ship.
   I am coming to you dearest.
Love and kisses,
Nic

November 16, 1911

Durres
Dearest,
   I arrived here with great difficulty. The fighting has been intense at times so I traveled only by night, hiding by day. There is much confusion in the city. Many are trying to leave. They don't care how! The trains are delayed more often than not and packed - standing room in the iron wagons only. No ships can be seen and the booking offices have been closed since I arrived. I heard tonight of a house where an agent lives. It is said that he will book passage from his house or at least that he has some ideas what ships are due here. I will try to see him tomorrow. We are still on the list for the Pindora, but there is no guarantee she will make port here.
   My heart - how I long for your arms, your caresses. Last Summer seems so distant now, though my memories of our embraces and love linger tauntingly. No artist could conceive of any sculpture that can compete with your naked body, shining wet in the water with such lovely and graceful curves. I remember well your laughter and how it made your tummy ripple.
   Speaking of your tummy - has the babe grown much? Does it kick? Oh, if I could only be with you tonight and kiss the babe right through your tummy - and your backside - and along your spine. Please sing to the babe tonight and pretend I am with you and can hear your sweet voice.
   You would laugh at my deluxe quarters. I am sleeping in a large fishing boat, with a very small bunk. I will have to rise before the moon goes down in case the fisherman wants his boat early and is the kind who whistles for the night patrol before he thinks. It is out of the wind and I have several blankets and the Sea to rock me to sleep.

   "The rest is about Albanian history," Arian commented. "He signs it,
Ever yours,
Nic

JOHANNA

"His Italian is better than mine," Johanna admitted. "I'll read the next one, dated 1911."

My Sweet Wife,
I'm safely outside the area where the fighting still goes on. I have found shelter with the church I told you about - the one with the children. However, they have to leave here soon - children and all. I would find it essential to help them relocate, but was wounded yesterday. Nothing to worry about - the saber hit my left leg and left a gash but when I got here one of the Sisters sewed it up. It will definitely slow me down, but I'll rest here a few days, then continue my journey to you.

There's plenty of dried fruit and cheese here and the church group must travel light. I have provisions and this is also a good place for a small group to hide. Those of us staying behind all have our injuries except a couple of lads we rescued weeks ago who refuse to leave us.

By the way, the baby I told you about lives. She is a girl and is safe now with the church group. We named her after you - Cassandra Elaine. She has your raven black hair. Well, actually, she is almost bald, but the wisps she does have are definitely black. I will miss her but not at all to the degree that I miss you. I know our baby will be even more beautiful with you as her Mother.

I long for you, dearest. You are my heart, my soul. Once we meet again, I will never part from you, even for a day. Not even an hour if that were possible, but certainly not for any frivolous reason - only when necessary to earn money for our keep. I have written my brother about us - I am certain he will sponsor us and help me find work. He has ever been my champion and friend.

I sleep in snatches now, even though there is no gunfire here to wake me. Sometimes it is the moans of my comrades who are recovering from their wounds, as am I. We have worked out chores so that each does what he can best do considering his injuries. The two lads I spoke of are

the only ones with us who are without wounds.
   Here I have lots of time to write, though I tire easily. I will sleep now and dream of you and write again soon.
Yours forever,
Nic

"He still had hope of health and travel, then." Arian said sadly. "The letter he wrote to me has never arrived. He probably sent it by pigeons and boys. It might make it to us still. I tried again to get news of him through the underground, but they knew nothing other than he had been injured rounding up orphans. It is hard to believe no one was at his deathbed, especially Erjon. The boy was devoted to Nic."

"Who is Erjon? The name is familiar somehow."

"Well that is a story for another night. Right now he is pretending to be Polish and stirring up revolutionaries in case the Germans occupy Poland. Erjon cannot be found. It wouldn't surprise me if Nic showed up with him."

JOHANNA

CHAPTER NINETEEN
CONNECTING ACROSS THE GREAT WATERS

    By the next evening Johanna and Arian had a plan. They would give serious thought on how to explain the events leading up to a grandson for these people in Greece. One option was to stay out of contact, but each felt that was a poor choice. They would someday have to tell Nicki and he might want to know his grandparents. Also, there might be some way they could trace his mother through ship records and find out more about the child. He actually had no birth certificate, only the one that really belonged to the unfortunate baby, Marie.
    "We had best consult a lawyer and ask that we be named legal guardians," Johanna observed.
    "We'll have plenty of time for that, but first we should consider a state marriage," Arian answered. "This isn't a romantic way to ask you, but we have both made a commitment to one another so it seems past the time for courtship."
    "Well past," giggled Johanna, thinking of all the formal, chaperoned walks and other formalities of English society. "I would love to join you in a state marriage. I have been happy with you without anything official but we should have less trouble getting guardianship for Nicki if our union is seen as legal. Also we may have other little ones coming along sooner than not."
    "Are you???"
    "Maybe. I've been waiting to tell you until I am sure, but yes, maybe."
    "Then you must see a physician this week!"

"A physician probably can't tell this early anymore than I can. I've been asking around and know of a great midwife. I delivered little Marie myself and she just shot out tiny thing that she was and two months early."

"I'll take a day off and go with you to the midwife whenever you think it is time. I want to learn what to do and I'll not leave you alone. No more will you have to birth a babe by yourself."

Nicki was beginning to make up for his quiet acceptance of any circumstance as a baby. He grew in size, in curiosity, in dexterity and in strength. Johanna could hardly lift him, but his agility made it seldom necessary. He had given up his naps weeks ago and from wake-up to bedtime he never stopped moving. He loved to watch Zack tumble and shadow box. Zack could even walk on his hands from the kitchen to the bedroom.

At night when Nicki finally tired he would cuddle up by Johanna and say, "Tell me story." His favorite story was about his Angel Mother.

"How about for a change I sit by Earth Mommy and you sit on my knee and I'll tell you about your Eagle Daddy who is high up in the sky?" Arian said on rare nights.

Indeed the man who sired Nicki was high in the sky atop a mountain so tall the only wild animals that chose to come there were the eagles. He was no longer confused and working daily to strengthen his leg for a trip down the mountain. He had been told that his love, Cassandra, had died aboard ship but he didn't believe it. The information only spurred him to more exertions to improve what muscle he had left in his debilitated leg.

Meanwhile, in the Bronx, plans proceeded with appointments for their official union and pre-birth exam. Their evenings, after Nicki went to sleep, were devoted mostly to work on the all important correspondence.

JOHANNA

"I think we need to make three copies," Ari said. "One to keep, one to send by regular post and one to send through the movement's courier bags. With all the skirmishes and plans for war in Europe I am not sure the regular post is reliable. In one of the letters to his wife, Niccolò said he had written me about the baby - a letter which never came."

"Could we please make a fourth copy in English? I have been meaning to let my parents know I am alive and well. Adding this epistle to my note would save me a lot of time explaining all over again."

"Yes, but could you wait to send it until after our state marriage? I don't want to get into an issue with your Father about making you honest. As if making you honest or honorable can only happen in a church ceremony. I never met a more honorable human being in my life."

Johanna carefully reread the letters from Niccolò. She chose three to send with the correspondence and saved the others for little Nicki when he was older. She diligently copied the three letters she was including in the packet so she could refer to any information within after she mailed the originals. She put only one of the original letters in the regular mail and the other two in the packet Arian was sending by special courier.

Next, Johanna made some sketches of the boy and some of his antics. The cutest one showed him trying to walk upside down like Zack. Arian and Zack joined her for breakfast and went over all she had written.

"Your Greek is better than you pretend," Arian remarked proudly.

"As we say in America, 'it's all Greek to me.'"

Arian grinned.

"All except these sketches. These are really special. I hate to part with them."

The couple chose April first as the date for their union. Johanna wanted to do the proper year of grieving for her lost family even though it seemed irrelevant so much had taken place. They married on what Johanna remembered as the date she was handed Nicki which she thought must also have been his birthday.

JOHANNA

CHAPTER TWENTY
PIATRA'S DISCOVERY
Northern Greece
Spring 1913

It was April and Isa Vladimar still had no word of his sister, Anastasia. Perhaps they were not traveling at all. They may have found a safe haven from the war going on all around. The Ottoman Empire had a finger hold on the region for ages. Serbia, Bulgaria, Montenegro, and Greece joined in a hotly contested war to drive out the Ottoman Empire and thus achieve recognition as sovereign countries. The battles were fought on numerous fronts. Troops had actually stomped over some of the grapes in Isa's vineyard. This war had been going on since October and it was now Spring.

Worse, the results from his efforts to find his older daughter, Cassandra, had brought only dreadful news. He spied Piatra, his younger daughter just coming down for breakfast. With his wife, Beatrice, away helping her aging parents in another part of Greece, Isa relied more and more on Piatra. Piatra was young but she was very efficient. In her own way she was better than her mother at the duties of running the household. She looked at things from a fresh viewpoint and took care of details. Beatrice would have been unnerved by the loss of several servants who found themselves in demand either as soldiers or keeping soldiers clothed and fed.

"Hopefully we will have a truce soon," Isa thought out loud. Isa had been appointed to a committee as one of three commissioners to assure adequate food for the civilian population of his district. This meant travel at least monthly and almost daily confused interactions with the telegraph service. Fortunately, they also employed homing pigeons which asked no questions and never talked back.

"Good morning, Poppa," the girl said, smiling. "Did the pigeons bring any news?"

"Only news relevant to my work as Commissioner of Nutrient Supplies. However, I have grown anxious about affairs at my sister's horse farm. She seems to have lost all reason traveling about among open warfare and neglecting things at home. Do we have a servant we could spare to go there and take a look?"

"It would be better if I go, Poppa. A servant would have no authority to step in if all is not well. Also, I would know if valuables are missing. I became quite familiar with Aunt's belongings when I visited all those summers growing up."

"Can you go and get back in two days time? The other commissioners are coming here the end of the week to go over supply lists and discuss priorities. They will be here overnight, perhaps longer, depending on knowledge regarding troop movements."

"Thank goodness for the pigeons," Piatra sighed. "Today and tomorrow should be clear around here unless Paulo is out hunting."

"I have a new stall tactic," Isa answered. "I ran across him at the Inn near Kastoria on my last trip. I approached him for a change. It was much to his surprise as he was seated with a young woman in his lap. I congratulated him on his new girlfriend and added, 'By the way I have heard that Cassandra and her aunt are alive and trying to get passage home from one of the islands. The war effort is making it difficult even though none of the Empire's fleets are equal to battle with the Grecian Naval Services.'

"Paulo's red face turned purple but I was out of there and gathering my escorts before he could get the woman off of his lap."

JOHANNA

When Piatra arrived at her aunt's house she found things organized and well kept by the caretakers. Browsing in the library for something to read she noticed a basket on the table that was overflowing with mail. She called the caretakers and asked about the basket of letters.

"We are authorized to open any business letters and to pay any amount past due. Her personal mail we leave for her to open when she returns."

"My aunt has been gone for months. I'll at least go through the letters and open those that seem to have a deadline or to be urgent."

Settled in a comfortable chair with tables on either side, Piatra sorted through the letters from oldest to most recent according to the stamps outside the envelopes. She uncovered one letter that was more like a package it was so thick. Curious Piatra surveyed it more closely.

This did not come through regular post, Piatra discovered. It obviously had arrived by courier. This could be urgent. It could even reveal the whereabouts of Anastasia and Anton. Anxiously she opened the package. Inside she found yet another sealed package. The only information on front of the second envelope was the words "Vladimar family."

"I am the Vladimar family or at least one of them." Piatra anxiously opened the package. For the next hour she was entranced, reading sections of the epistle over and over.

"When Poppa sees this he'll be apoplectic," she mumbled to herself. "He will want to go immediately to America and bring the baby back. I see lots of frantic activity in the future. Maybe that will save me."

Piatra munched on the pear she had placed in her pocket. She casually glanced through the other mail and saw a second package this one delivered by regular post. "They wrote twice," she muttered. Apparently they wrote two letters but why would they send one by post and the other by courier. Briefly looking at the contents Piatra noticed they were the same except for the letters to her sister.

"Well it looks like they just didn't trust either mail service. I wonder who the courier was and where he was from. Maybe it was Erjon."

Wishing she had come to her aunt's house earlier, Piatra supplied herself with pen and paper and settled in front of the desk.

Dear Johanna and Arian, (Excuse me but do you have the same last name? Should I say the Zantos family???)

First I want to thank you for writing us. We don't know where Anastasia is. She seems to have disappeared along with my sister Cassandra and Anton, our stable manager. Your information confirms what my father's investigations revealed. However the circumstances of death are hard to believe, even though the ship's captain wrote an affidavit saying it was all true. Cassandra simply would not have done those things they said about her. We believe she died of foul play. The captain is part of a cover-up Poppa thinks.

I will not see my mother and father for a few more days as both are traveling. I'm kind of hiding out here from the man that Poppa wants me to marry. He was intended for Cassandra but she flew the coop, as you know.

Since I'm only 14 and just barely that, I don't want to marry anyone. This old man is the cousin of Poppa and owns some land Poppa wants. He argues that since Cassandra was betrothed to him the least a father can do is promise the younger daughter, which unfortunately turns out to be me.

Now that I have your letters, I am not quite as anxious. When I show them to Poppa he will be so upset he probably won't even speak to anyone until he can get to New York. He can't 'give me away' at a wedding if he is in America. Maybe you can get a lawyer so he will need to be there a long time.

Do you want the baby? Do you think Cassandra wanted you to have him? I don't think she wanted Poppa to have him. They used to be so close I was almost jealous. Since

JOHANNA

Poppa decided Cassandra should marry this old man I told you about they are not on speaking terms. Poppa says Cassandra is disowned and I have no sister. I still can't believe she is dead. The only question I have is, why doesn't she write me like she promised?

Anastasia and Anton smuggled Cassandra out of Greece. We know she took a ship to America and the ship line people say she never got there but died alone in her cabin of an overdose.

Now, why she should do that? It had to be that she didn't know what she was drinking. Someone must have drugged her and taken her money. I know she had money – I gave her all of my savings and so did mama. Besides that Erjon who brought her the news from – oh I forget his name – her lover, he brought money also in a blue velvet purse. I don't know where she put the money but I found the purse in her room empty. I keep the purse among my most treasured things. I guess it reminds me of my sister and days all gone. Of course it could have held diamonds but it smelled like coins.

Anyway we will get back to you after I see Mama and Poppa. I just wanted you to know that we got your letters – both of them. They are just alike? Why did you send two?

By the way if you should hear from Erjon, tell him I call in his debt. He promised that if I ever needed him he would be here. I need him before the middle of June to make sure that Paulo and I do not marry. He can help me escape or better still advise me on how to make Paulo go away. I know that sounds drastic but these are drastic times and I'm afraid to be with Paulo.

Oh I didn't say before I don't think. Paulo's the old cousin that was betrothed to Cassandra and now to me. Ugghg! It makes me sick to think about it. Momma's name is Beatrice and Poppa's is Isa. I am Platra and we three are all the family until you told us about the baby you call Nicki. Of course if Cassandra IS alive that would make 5 of us.

Also if you could send a picture of the baby that would

be great. The sketches are cute but I'd also like a real picture. To be sure I get it, send it to Piatra Vladimar at the return address on the envelope.
The baby's aunt, Piatra, goodbye now.
Oh, and I didn't mean that part about drastic stuff.

JOHANNA

CHAPTER TWENTY-ONE
SHADOWS IN THE WIND

Piatra hurriedly saddled her horse. The groomsman who had accompanied her here was no where to be seen. She had to go to the nearby village to post her response. That's probably where he was. In all fairness she had thought to stay through the night so the man was not really neglecting his duty. Not finding him in the village she had two choices. She could go back to the villa and spend the night. Or - she could head straight for home. Piatra covered her long jet black braid with her coat and pulled the cap out of her pocket, not even giving thought to danger ahead.

Over half way home the wind picked up, bringing with it moist air and occasional flecks of ice. There was no need to urge her mare onward. The horse was as anxious as Piatra to get to cover. When they came to a rocky slope, she slowed the horse.

"Careful here. These stones could hobble you."

As they slowed down Piatra noticed a shadow up ahead - a lone figure - or perhaps a boulder. They were off the path. Somehow they had veered eastward and Piatra was looking at a cliff though not a very high one. It was disguised by scrub trees and large rocks but her eyes now accustomed to the ever darkening night she could see enough to turn her horse to the west.

"Oh! Who goes there?" Piatra said as the movement of a stallion right next to her mare startled her. He and his rider could have no good intention with such stealth.

"It is you, Piatra. It is like you to be out in the dead of night all alone. I have been following you. Do you know the secret caves ahead?"

"Erjon! I just called for you. But I wrote the request on a letter I posted less than an hour ago. You couldn't possibly know."

"You're in need of me then? Well, here I am as promised."

"Not tonight. Mid-June. Paulo has a written agreement signed by Poppa to wed me on the fifteenth. Poppa regrets agreeing but I am afraid he is legally and morally bound. Will you whisk me away like you did Cassandra?"

"I made a great mistake with Cassandra. I left her to take on other challenges when we reached the train station. She had all her papers and tickets to sail first class on the Leona II. I should have shadowed her all the way to Arian's."

"They tell us she was taking some kind of drugs. They said she was despondent when locked in her cabin after attacking two of the crew members. Can you imagine such a story as that? We don't believe it."

"Neither do I." Erjon replied. "Come though. It will be heavy rain soon and cold icy rain. Follow me, I know a shortcut through this rocky terrain."

Almost an hour later Piatra found herself on the edge of their vineyard. She looked all around but could not see Erjon. The rain had completely stopped this side of the mountain foothills and the moon was peeking through the clouds to guide her.

Piatra was never sure if Erjon was with her or if she imagined his presence on the lonely path that night.

Piatra slept most of the morning after her long night ride. She had difficulty falling asleep as she pondered on when to tell Poppa about the baby. He had so many depending on him now and would want to leave immediately.

On awakening she decided not to take the information straight to her father. He was in his library going over data for the meeting scheduled with his co-commissioners and had left word with the staff that he was not to be disturbed until the guests arrived. She sorted through the correspondence again.

"I wish Momma were here. Poppa will be so upset," Piatra said aloud, a little afraid of her father's anticipated rage. "Should I tell him about the baby first or the elopement? I don't understand when Cassandra could have gotten married. It must have been near here but I should have been there. She must not have trusted me, her own sister. I would have kept her secret like it was precious as gold." Piatra wiped a tear from her eye.

Piatra went first to the kitchen. She had enjoyed a friendly, casual relationship with 'Cookie,' as she called their resident chef. This began when she first learned to walk. She loved tottering to the kitchen, following the enticing smells.

After eating heartily she went out to the stables to see about Misty, her mare. She had ridden the horse hard and late giving her only a sketchy grooming on her return due to the late hour. She wanted to personally groom the mare this morning as she felt she had short changed Misty the night before. It was too stormy or she could stand a good ride to clear her thinking.

One of the other commissioners for foods came in from the storm that was brewing outside, accompanied by Isa's trusted lawyer, Hector Kryellis.

Isa greeted the newcomers himself. He had been waiting for them.

"Let's wait a while for our third commissioner and for my daughter. She will want to hear any news of her sister," Isa began. "Why don't you freshen up and we'll have dinner."

Before they left the dinner table the third commissioner arrived.

With Piatra as recorder the three commissioners completed their review of the supplies and needs for feeding the populace. The Balkan War was in its sixth month and there were shortages, but the importations of fresh supplies from Italy had helped keep things manageable.

"I have some news of your daughter," one of the Commissioners said. "The woman who died in a skirmish with some of the ship's crew may not have been your daughter, Cassandra, at all. My friend who is a private detective was able to find and talk to three of the crew of the Leona II. He spoke with each separately and they each described the woman as unusually short and large-boned. Her most noticeable features were her missing front tooth and a nose that had been broken and healed slightly crooked. Of course that could have happened since you last saw your daughter, but the way they described the nose they indicated it looked to them like the breakage had occurred during the developmental years."

"I have news also that I found at Aunt Anastasia's." Piatra just blurted it out, unable to hold her tongue another second. "A man who says he is the brother of the man Cassandra fell in love with wrote along with a woman who claims she has Cassandra's baby."

Isa rose and roared like a lion. "What did you just say? Cassandra wasn't married. And a baby! These must be ruffians wanting money from us. Where are they; I'll have them arrested and interrogated."

"That's a lot of news to spring on your father all at once," Hector intervened. "Perhaps you could tell us what you found that made you believe this story - if you do believe."

"Well, I knew Cassandra had a lover, but only after a messenger came to her with money and a letter telling her the lover had died. The letter told her to go to America and his brother would help her."

"How did you know such a thing?"

"Well, for one, I met the messenger. I am ashamed to tell you the other way I knew. I sneaked into her room and read the letter she was writing to the brother about would

JOHANNA

he meet her ship or some such - I don't remember exactly. Momma had found out that Cassandra was pregnant - or maybe she just guessed by the look of her tummy. I think that is why Aunt came here - I think Momma summoned her."

Hector broke in once again.

"Then that settles it. If Cassandra was pregnant and showing when she disappeared with Anastasia she would have definitely been showing on the ship and not at all a match with the woman just described. She must have resold her steamship tickets and gone somewhere with Anastasia to have the baby."

Piatra looked at her father's whitening face and pained eyes.

"The servants will serve drinks and light desserts in the parlor," Piatra spoke quietly. "Perhaps you would give me some time alone with my father. I returned with this correspondence long past midnight and either I was sleeping or he was in seclusion here in the library. I really must go over this with him alone and then he can discuss the situation with you when he is over the shock."

As Piatra read from the letters and shared her analysis of the situation, Isa became morose, then angry, then happy - so happy he laughed aloud in a glorious, deep fulfilling laugh.

"I have a Grandson - I have an heir that will carry our name into the future. Oh, what a fool I've been. Why didn't I see the situation and take Cassandra in my arms. I cherish the child already! All I have to do now is go to America and retrieve the boy. Piatra, make travel arrangements immediately. You are coming with me - I'll need help with the baby on the ship back."

"Are you sure we can just go and pick up the baby? After all he is with his uncle."

"Of course I can. Any judge would agree. We'll find Cassandra and bring her home. That woman must have stolen her identity. She'll come home and raise the baby with our help. Meanwhile we'll get legal guardianship. Hector can start the process right away! Where is Hector?"

"Hector - Hector - best of news!" he bellowed.

JOHANNA

CHAPTER TWENTY-TWO
SPLENDOR IN THE BRONX
The Bronx, New York
Spring, Summer and Fall, 1913

Intimacy with Arian was something Johanna had longed for during her first nine months in America. They shared a baby, an apartment, plans for their future as landlords, dinners and breakfasts, sight-seeing outings - everything that matters except a bed. By the time they finally found themselves frantically shedding clothing, both were caught up in incredible passion.

This first time set the stage for multiple nights to come. If Arian so much as touched her, she shivered all over in anticipation and desire. Each night after Nicki's story hour, Johanna put him to bed while Arian showered with his ingeniously rigged spray nozzle. He then ran a warm bath for Johanna. When Johanna stepped out of the tub, an unclothed Arian would be there with towels. He dried her with one; her body trembling with need. Wrapped in the largest towel, Johanna was lifted in the air and taken directly to Arian's bed. It would be hard to say who took the initiative once they arrived. Johanna preferred the nights that there was little foreplay. She seemed to be constantly ready and the activity with the towels was enough to drive her mad for Arian's entry into her very being.

This is what it's like to make love with someone you truly love, she thought. With Arian I have lust and love, tenderness and excitement.

Temporarily satisfied, the two would dress in pajamas or whatever seemed comfortable for the weather that evening. The next hour was devoted to adult communication. It was time to discuss tenants, repairs, shopping needs, correspondence - whatever either of them brought to attention. They dealt with the issues or agreed to table some to await more information or more thought.

The rest of the evening was devoted to togetherness. If they lit candles and opened wine the stage was set for a romantic evening inevitably leading back to the bed. Often, they found a radio station playing dance music. Johanna discovered a shop with lace and sheer fabrics left over from an establishment specializing in bridal gowns. She fashioned romantic outfits for herself; one especially revealing in enticing places. They danced barefoot. Arian danced shirtless.

Other nights one would suggest a game of poker or they would bring out the checkers. Loser must kiss the winner. One day Johanna had an idea to dress up for the game. At a second-hand store she had found a starched dickey and white bow tie like the gentlemen callers in London wore to debutante parties, dinners and other gatherings. After they finished with the business of the day she stretched.

"Are you in the mood for poker," she asked.

"Only if you won't be peeved when I win."

"You get the cards. I'll be right back."

When Johanna reappeared she was wearing a black, slinky skirt - one much shorter than the ankle length style of the times. She had on nothing else except the dicky and the white bow tie.

"Unfair," Arian said. "How can I concentrate on the cards?"

They played little poker that night. Most of the nights they didn't dance or play a game; they cooked instead. Arian had always wanted to own a restaurant and serve exotic concoctions of his own creation, using basic ingredients from his Mediterranean childhood. They experimented in the kitchen. When something wasn't edible they had food fights. Afterward both had to rush to stand together in the tub and spray well.

JOHANNA

CHAPTER TWENTY-THREE
AMAZING NEWS
October 1913

Johanna continued off and on to question Zack about his earlier living arrangements. No matter how she approached the subject however, Zack would not answer directly. All he would say is

"It's much better not to talk about it," or "I don't even want to think about it."

One day, therefore, she was surprised when he said he had a brother.

"At least I think I have. My mother claims him, but he is not like me."

"Can you bring him here? I would like to meet him."

"I don't know. I think they don't want him out on the streets."

"Then I will go to see him. When shall we plan the trip? How far is it?"

Zack spoke forcefully. "Now that's impossible. You cannot go there and especially you cannot take Nicki there. In a year or two my brother can come to see you perhaps. Meanwhile, he makes beautiful carvings. I wonder if you could send him work to do. He likes to carve animals especially, but he can do boats, lighthouses and a few other kinds of houses. He could make wooden toys for the baby. Maybe a train with several cars. He would not charge much."

"Certainly we can give it a try," Johanna said. "Does he have his own wood and tools?"

"He has a pocket knife he uses. He just seems to see the image of what he's making in the wood. Watching him is amazing."

"Tomorrow buy one of those little inexpensive Albanian flags. See if your brother can carve a two headed Eagle, like on the flag."

That night Johanna spoke to Arian about the conversation with Zack.

"It sounds like his brother does live in a brothel." Arian commented. "That would explain why he reacted so forcefully to your suggestion of going there. It is well known that when a working woman there gets pregnant the ladies take care of the baby boys through toddlerhood and later on depending on the boy and when they believe he can make it on his own. The girls they keep until they are old enough to work there."

"How disgusting," Johanna remarked.

"Since prostitution is illegal there are no guide lines or checks on the procedures of the houses. I'm afraid legalizing them is out of the question in this country for a long, long time. With that kind of business, babies are inevitable."

Arian continued, "While we're on such serious topics I have news to share with you. Someone from the group I belong to that is helping to make sure that the freedom of Albania is intact arrived from Europe today. According to him Erjon is not really a boy, but a young man who is small in stature and goes undercover as a boy quite often. He was the messenger who brought news of Arian's condition to Cassandra. Since then he's been back in the area of the Vladimar Vineyards several times. Actually he led and coordinated the raid that recovered the guns and ammunition that had been stolen from our supply line.

"If you remember, Niccolò had found the perpetrator and his hiding place but needed a team and transport to go in and retrieve the merchandise."

"It must have been a foreboding task to be given to such a young man," Johanna said.

"I never met Erjon but I knew that he was a close

colleague of Niccolò. Niccolò actually trained him in the same ways that I trained Niccolò. I am told that Erjon mastered the techniques of stealth and deceit like no other. As a very young boy he had experience as an acrobat in the circus - a traveling one performed mostly by gypsies. He is limber and astute and works mostly out of trees like Niccolò and I. It is remarkable how people, even very careful ones, almost never look up into a tree to see if danger lurks there."

"Really, you climbed up in trees to get information or to attack people? I would doubtless be one of those who doesn't look up, I'm afraid," Johanna admitted.

Arian smiled in a most provocative way.

"Perhaps I could train you," he grinned.

"Back to serious, though. According to this man who arrived today, there is an outside chance that Niccolò is alive. I'm not to get my hopes up because it's only about a twenty percent chance that one of the rescued men was him.

"This traveler has spoken personally to Erjon, who swears that after he left Cassandra he went back to the caves near the church and found no men and no graves newer than the ones he had seen there before.

"He sought out a monk who he had met while traveling with Cassandra and found the monk had heard of a party of wounded men being taken to a monastery located high in the mountains and almost inaccessible. There were ten men that began the journey and seven that made it to the monastery.

"They were being taken there because a famous physician might be able to help them. All seven were critically ill with ulcerated wounds, flu, pneumonia and goodness only knows what else. On the journey up the mountain only one was heard to speak. He was delirious and called out the name of a goddess. Erjon thought it must be Cassandra. If true it means that Niccolò was alive and being treated by the most skilled physician on the continent, possibly on any continent. He uses both the methods common in Christian areas and those of the Middle East and tribes native to the Americas."

"Oh Arian how wonderful. If only we could have such news about Cassandra. However, I'm afraid that she was buried at sea from the information I was given there. I so hope your brother is alive."

"I'm trying to take this news calmly. However I feel like celebrating. Would you like to light a candle and open a bottle of wine?"

"I'll get the candle if you get the wine," she replied enthusiastically. As Johanna rose she felt a huge contraction.

"Uh, Arian, would you mind getting the midwife instead of the wine?"

Arian returned almost immediately.

"I saw Zack and sent him to get Jessica. I'm not letting you deliver this baby alone." Arian put his arms tenderly around Johanna.

"I'm so grateful you are here with me," Johanna said as she leaned into his embrace.

Zack and Jessica Larkin arrived in only a few minutes.

"Can I do anything else to help?" Zack asked.

"Squat down Johanna," directed Jessica. "Arian, wash your hands, then pull up a chair and sit behind her and hold her. Zack, start some water boiling and wash your hands."

Jessica checked Johanna's pelvis and determined that the baby was in position for delivery. "Everything looks good. Just breathe slowly now and pant when the next contraction comes."

"Pant?" Johanna said.

"It seems to help," Jessica replied. "I had one mother do it and it helped so much that now I tell all mothers to do it."

"Should I do anything special?" Arian asked.

"Just support her and remind her to breathe. If she gets too tired it'll be hard for her to stay squatting but it's the best position to deliver in. You need to keep her upright."

JOHANNA

"The water is boiling," Zack told Jessica.

"Good. Rinse a pan thoroughly with some of it then pour the water out and put the rest of the water in and let it start cooling. Then boil some more. Johanna did you boil some towels like I asked?"

"Yes I did, they're in the top dresser drawer wrapped in a boiled sheet."

"Good. Zack, once you start more water can you get the sheet? Don't open it yet though. We want to keep the towels as clean as possible."

Zack made quick work of rinsing and refilling the pan then got the sheet covered bundle. "Here you go," he said as he put the sheet next to Jessica with the opening at the top.

Jessica smiled her thanks at Zack while she helped Johanna through another contraction. "You're very close now. I want you to start pushing during the contractions."

Soon the baby's first cries told the world of her arrival.

Arian jumped up and started dancing with Jessica as Johanna lay back exhausted but smiling tenderly at the wrapped babe in her arms. Zack stood watching his friends, a smile on his face.

Nicki woke up and joined the festivities. "I have a brother! I have a brother!"

Johanna motioned for Nicki to come to her side. She uncovered the baby's face and arm for him to touch.

"You're almost right," Johanna said. "You have a sister. The baby is a little girl."

"A girl?" Nicki asked. "Do girls like to play?"

"Yes, but she won't be old enough to play games for a while. But you can still help me take care of her."

"What is her name?" Nicki asked.

"That's a good question, Nicki. What do you think, Arian?"

"We could name her after your mother. Would you like that?" Arian said as he swung a protesting Jessica in a circle.

"I'd never name a child after my mother," Johanna shuddered. "I want to name her after you. How about Ariana?"

Arian looked a little startled. "I would be honored," he said as he released Jessica to come kiss his wife.

JOHANNA

CHAPTER TWENTY-FOUR
HOMES NEEDED
Fall 1913

Johanna was determined to learn more about Zack and the life he lived before he was on the streets. It was hard for Johanna to believe that he had lived in a brothel but it did seem to be true. The carvings Zack brought from his brother were spectacular. Even though Johanna was helping with the sale of the carvings Zack still dodged questions about where he had lived before trying to survive on the streets. She continued to worry about his brother and other children in the same situation.

Her instincts told her that something should be done but how could she help since she wasn't even a citizen of this country.

One day she saw a group of women walking with signs 'GIVE WOMEN THE VOTE'. Johanna followed them to the corner where one of the women gave a short speech. She emphasized the corruption that women could help decrease if only they had the power of the vote. When the talk was over Johanna approached the speaker.

"I have heard that children live in the brothels. Do you think that's true?"

"Sadly I do believe it is," the woman replied. "Children are the natural result of the activities there and there are few places that will take the babies. Sometimes the mothers keep them for as long as they can, hoping to help them live at least until time to be weaned. Then they leave them on a church doorstep. Members of the congregation sometimes take them to their homes. The lucky ones are absorbed into the family. The unlucky ones are used as servants. Perhaps I should say misused. They tell me even very young children can polish shoes and scrub pots and pans. Some of those not taken by a family end up in an orphanage. Some die from exposure to the elements before being found. Those not left by a church, well, it's hard to think about it."

"Is there anything I could do to help the situation," Johanna asked.

"You could take a baby. They need homes and good ones. It is unspeakable to say what happens to them as they grow older if they're still living in the brothel."

Johanna could hardly wait until Arian would be home. She was fascinated by the idea of getting another baby. It would be like having twins since their own Ariana was only a few weeks old. The baby she and Arian had made with love was adorable. With their own baby so young, would Arian agree?

After Nicki's bedtime story Johanna and Arian tucked him in together, then went to the kitchen for their evening discussion.

"I have something serious to bring up tonight," Johanna said as she brought out the tea. "I talked to one of the women speaking at a woman's rights gathering and she says the babies from the brothels are often left at a church doorstep before they can hold up their heads. If I'm going to talk other women into taking babies I need to set an example. Would you be willing to take a baby?"

Arian laughed.

"It seems Zack has just adopted at least one boy, aged about twelve. According to the grocer he is stealing food again."

"I noticed some food missing from here, too. I thought Zack had started being honest with us. I guess he still doesn't trust us."

"Well, to give him some credit he probably doesn't trust anyone. I'm guessing he doubts that we would be willing to

JOHANNA

supply more kids with food. Not many people would be willing. I gave the grocer money but I'm going to talk to Zack about being straight with us."

"But you haven't answered my question. Would you be willing to take a baby?"

"I am still getting use to Ariana. Maybe we could approach this in a different way. Have you thought about how you would connect people with babies?"

"I thought perhaps Zack would help me. If he could get someone in the brothel to bring babies to a certain location we can have the potential parents meet them there. If we can only get one or two physicians to help us we can even have the babies checked out by a nurse."

"Our adopting one baby hardly makes a difference. If you can get some mothers to run it, we can set up ground floor space in that six-story we are just closing on. They can set up a business of some sort as a cover and have an apartment size area for the babies and toddlers to stay while families are recruited. We will be a while redoing the rest of the first floor as the last tenants ripped out the piping and knocked holes in a couple of walls. Maybe that is good because if this really takes hold, we will need to make several dormitory type rooms for babies and mothers to be together."

Johanna answered excitedly.

"That's a much better plan than a meeting for a few minutes. Potential mothers can even go in and play with the babies before taking them for good."

Thoughtful, Arian considered his words.

"First you had best find out if the women of the brothel will run a business and a safe house. Shall we ask Zack to invite some of his 'brothers and sisters' to dinner. They can then see if the idea has any support among the mothers."

"Italian will be quicker than anything else - I'll put on a big pot of pasta and make an Alfredo sauce. When you talk to Zack, see if the butcher down the street has anything we can throw in it to make it hearty. I have onion and carrots here."

Arian laughed again.

"You mean for tomorrow's dinner? We'll talk to Zack tonight, though."

"Maybe our focus should first be on the pregnant ladies," Johanna said thoughtfully. "They must be frightened and at a loss who to turn to for help."

"Some might want to keep their babies and leave the brothels," Arian added. "There could be some among them who would sleep in the refuge home, help with the business and babies, and keep their little ones with them while they learned skills to earn money in less harsh ways than they have now."

"I'll teach piano and needlework. The piano lessons would be for fun, but some could earn a living doing embroidery, mending and garment making."

Arian nodded.

"Some could be trained as house maids, or receptionists in offices. There are lots of possibilities. Joule has a cousin who has a message delivery service. He might be willing to employ some. He is forever complaining about difficulty in finding reliable help."

"It is getting late," Johanna replied. "If we're going to talk to Zack tonight you had best find him. Thank you for helping with this endeavor. I think you're right. Our taking one baby is not as worthwhile as getting the ball rolling. We can save dozens of babies and women."

JOHANNA

CHAPTER TWENTY-FIVE
PIE HALL

Zack was skeptical.

"Sure, something should be done. But the houses are well-protected if by no other way than the list of customers who don't want to see their names in the newspaper."

"We aren't planning to expose people or to tell anyone what to do. We just want to know if any mothers in the houses want to help us get homes for their youngsters? They certainly have alternatives. Orphan trains are leaving regularly filled with street children," Johanna pleaded. "Don't you think one or two would come for dinner?"

"That is a busy time for the women. I could bring a dozen hungry boys."

"Yes, then, bring the boys. Some of them will tell the women, undoubtedly."

"Maybe," Zack cautioned. "If certain people hear they slipped out of the house they may be whipped; most likely though no one will notice, as is usual. I think they are allowed out after dark because the clientele doesn't want to 'see' them. If a boy said he had been to a dinner party, the others would think he was either kidding or caught a rat."

"I was going to make a stew. I think instead I'll have sliced beef and baked potatoes with spinach soup and fresh baked bread."

"Your odds of getting boys here just went up. How about a great big apple cobbler for desert?"

Maybe it was the warm night. Maybe it was the moonlight. Maybe it was the promise of apple cobbler.

However, there was no maybe about hungry boys. They started drifting in about an hour before the appointed time. When the count got to ten, Johanna added water to the spinach soup and boiled all the pasta in the house. She sent Zack to the butcher's and appointed Arian chief cook so she could talk to the boys. Twenty-two arrived and ate; six stayed to discuss Johanna's plan.

"Thanks for coming Ricky," Zack called to one of the larger boys as they left the building.
"Good food, thanks for letting me in on this," Ricky replied.
"See you later," Zack said as they parted.
Ricky walked briskly because of the cool temperature. When he came to the park he decided to cut through even though it was dark.
People often hid between the hedges when they were hungry and wanted to cop a few coins. The boy started to whistle as he walked cautiously. Suddenly he heard a second noise, different from his. It was coming from the right and drawing Ricky toward it.
Someone was in pain, moaning and gasping. Ricky knew that the rules of survival said to stay out of things that don't involve you. However, curiosity got the best of him. He headed toward the sound.
Ricky approached slowly hoping it was not a trap. When he came close enough in the dim light of the moon he saw a thin figure. Well part of her was thin. She was squatting over her knees and completely naked except for shoes.
"Whew!" said Ricky. "What have we here?"
A female voice answered him. "Please help me. Please." Suddenly the woman started gasping; taking very deep breaths.
At that point Ricky realized she was having a baby and seemed about to birth. All Ricky could think to do was go to the woman who not an hour ago was serving pie.
Not stopping to remember that he never got involved in

anything other than himself he decided to help this woman get to the pie lady.

"I can't help you but I know someone who can. Come with me. Can you walk?" the youth asked.

"I don't know. I don't think for very far," the young woman said.

"Do you have a cloak or anything around here to wear?" Ricky asked.

"I stole two towels and put them and what I was wearing in a laundry bag. It's over there. I didn't want the birth to mess up my only clothes," she replied.

"I don't have many clothes either, but let's wrap you in my jacket so it looks like I'm carrying laundry. Can you get on my back?"

"I'm way too big to do that."

"Let's try this," Ricky kneeled on the ground. "Sit on my shoulders and straddle my neck."

The young woman did so and Ricky forced himself up. Fortunately it was not far from the park to the Zantos' apartment.

A frantic knock at Arian and Johanna's door revealed a two-headed person. Both heads were talking incoherently. When untangled the heads resolved into one of the boys from the supper and a very pregnant young woman.

"You can help her, can't you?" pleaded the boy.

"Please, if you can help my baby live I'll do anything," the young woman seconded the plea. She was shivering heavily, her skin blue with cold.

"Yes, but I'll need your help," Johanna told the boy. "Start by building a fire in the stove and boiling some water. Arian you need to work in the morning. Try to get some sleep."

"I'll go for the midwife first," Arian said.

Johanna made a pot of herb tea for the young woman and made her as comfortable as possible.

Arian came back in a few minutes with Jessica. Jessica,

seeing the boy boiling the water directed him and Johanna. "Arian, get her a blanket and warm it at the stove. Johanna, hold that cup for her, she's shivering too much to do so herself. You Boy, wash your hands. What's your name girl?"

"I'm Rita, Rita Starr. That isn't my real name; it is the one they call me by. I don't dare tell you my real name. My father would find me and shoot everyone in the house.

"Please, you'll help my baby to live? I don't want him to die. Since I've been at the house three out of the four babies delivered died while being born. The midwife that comes frightens me. She tells me I am too young to be a mother; that I carry a devil child."

"What nonsense," Jessica interrupted, her smiling green eyes flashing with impatience. "You are young, but I've birthed healthy children to younger mothers. As for a 'devil child,' well there's no such thing. You just relax and listen to me. We'll have your son or daughter in your arms as soon as soon may be."

"You are very kind. I think God must have been smiling on me when this boy found me and brought me here."

Johanna, seeing Jessica had matters in hand with the boy assisting her went to the piano and started playing Brahm's Lullaby to soothe the younger woman.

The baby was well on the way but its arrival was still an hour or two away. In between contractions the group talked.

"Thank you so much for bringing me here young man," said Rita to the boy. "I don't think I can ever thank you enough. My name is Rita, what's yours?"

"They mostly call me 'Hey You,' but Mama called me Ricky. You can call me Ricky or Rick if you want."

"How did you know that they would help me, Rick?" Rita drew the youth out.

"I had dinner here earlier. We talked about starting a place for the babies that aren't wanted. And we had pie. The best pie I ever had," he said.

"When this is over we might just have a piece left over for you Rick," said Johanna. "Would you be interested in a

JOHANNA

place to stay Rita? At least until you decide where you want to go?"

"Do I get to keep my baby?" Rita asked.

"Of course you do if you want to," Johanna said. "But if you want to go back to the house we'll try to find a home for it. That's what we were talking to Rick about. A place where the babies can find parents if the mothers want to keep working and the mothers who want to go into a different profession can get training and watch the extra little ones until they find homes."

"I never want to go back," said Rita.

Jessica, who had been following the conversation with interest smiled and nodded at this.

"I'm going to train some of the women to be midwives. Not all of them, mind. Only the ones with the talent. And I know we haven't talked about this Johanna, but I'm helping with this project."

"I'll be grateful for your assistance, Widow Larkin," Johanna said formally.

Jessica cackled. "Might could use some strong young'uns to help walk the women and do some cleaning."

"How would you choose who would get to do that?" asked Rick.

"Well, we need several trustworthy boys who are willing to work. Some would do carpentry, some painting and some chores that I haven't thought of yet. Also, we need boys who will stay at the Hall. Just being there will deter troublemakers. Make the troublemakers stay away," Johanna clarified when she saw Rick's look of confusion. "If you know anyone who would be interested, my husband and I would like to meet them. If they don't know how to do the work but want to learn we can teach them."

"If I do that, do I work for my meals?" Rick asked. "I've got a place I can sleep dry. But, Man, I would love food every day?"

"I'm afraid you'd have to give up your place if you wanted to work as a security guard for us. We'd need you to live at the Hall where the women and babies will live. You'd have your own bed in a dormitory at first. Eventually you'd have a room of your own. But, we haven't built them yet. That's why we need boys who can do or learn carpentry and painting. Even after the rooms are finished I think there will be enough work for these boys to stay on. We'd like them to live at the Hall, too, if at all possible in case a repair is needed.

"No one will have to stay there all the time though. We'll get two to six boys who can do each job so they can take shifts. We'd like all of them to be willing to walk with mothers in labor too. That way there'll always be someone to get a midwife and someone to stay with the mother."

"If we run out of work in the Hall for the carpenters and painters I have plenty in the apartments," Arian added. "If I start another pie now it'll be ready about the time the baby is, apple or peach this time?"

About half hour later a little boy with great lungs woke Nicki and Ariana. Nicki using his best grown persona proceeded to drag out the small tin tub that was once his and was now used by Ariana.

Arian brought his daughter to Johanna to nurse after he changed her diaper. The apple pie was shared by all.

By mid-afternoon the next day Rita and baby Edward were situated in one of the unfinished rooms of what was to become a home for homeless Mothers.

Rick had walked over with her carrying her laundry bag of towels, a half smile on his face. The smile was partly for the promise of plenty of pie and mostly for the promise of the closest thing he'd ever known to a family.

So this was the beginning of Pie Hall. Rita not only agreed to leave the brothel and help set up the home, but to help run the cover business in the front of the building.

JOHANNA

CHAPTER TWENTY-SIX
BLOOD TIES
New York City
1914

The warlike activity all around Europe delayed Isa's trip to New York, but he was determined to go and bring back his grandson. Little communication had come from the Americans about his grandchild: two pictures and three or four letters.

He had finally accepted Cassandra's death as a fact. The two private investigators he hired learned the ship's name from Johanna. Anastasia had given them still another name. The Mathilda showed no Cassandra Vladimar as boarding, but the Leona II had such a booking.

The P.I.s went so far as to interview a few first-class passengers from both ships who were still in the New York City area. Finally they found a woman who had sailed on the Leona II. She definitely remembered the girl who had called herself Cassandra.

"She was a sneaky thief. She paired up with one of the seamen and drew crowds to watch her fantastic pantomimes while he took jewelry and money from the cabins."

"Doesn't sound like anyone we are looking for, but do you remember whether she was pregnant and pretty far along?"

"Not a chance!"

"What happened to her?"

"When the jewelry was found in her cabin, she pulled a knife on the seaman assigned to investigate. She died in the struggle and he came away with scratches... either that or she was thrown to the sharks, which some believed."

Going back to records of the Mathilda, the P.I. found a long death list, including the name 'Sophia Corleono: *Died in childbirth*.'

"We have come to believe this Sophia must have stolen or perhaps bought your daughter's first-class tickets and then used your daughter's name because it was on the paperwork. That explains why, although your sister bought first-class tickets, Johanna Zantos says Cassandra was in steerage. It also fits with the information that our private investigator reported from the Sicilian port city, Palermo, regarding lodgings. This was the port from which both the Leona II and Matilda departed. The P.I. has a signed affidavit certifying that both a Cassandra Zantos and a Sophia Corleono rented lodgings at the same rooming house the Winter of 1912."

When he finally got away, Isa took an ocean steamer. He was seasick throughout the voyage. Again he cursed himself for sending Cassandra away.

When Johanna actually received dates for Isa's arrival she became concerned. The letter received from Piatra indicated that he would want Nicki. From reading what Piatra wrote he seemed to be a man used to getting his own way. What if he was alone with the boy and just took him. Johanna knew that the guardianship request that she and Arian submitted was approved by the U.S. However she had not heard any news regarding Isa's claim.

"I want one of the three of us to be with them all the time." Johanna remarked to Arian and Zack. "He could just walk out of here with him and we would never see Nicki again."

"I think you are being reasonable," Arian said. "The first week we will be very careful. Then we will evaluate further. Mind you, though, you'll probably get opposition regarding alone time with Nicki. He'll want to take the boy to the apartment we set up for Isa's use."

JOHANNA

"That is a perfect place for him to plan escape. I say we don't use the apartment. Nicki is outgrowing his baby bed. Let's go out right now and buy a trundle bed. We can use the upper one with the lower hidden when Isa leaves. While he's here he can share Nicki's room. Nicki will be safer that way."

Arian met Isa's ship, and a tired and out of sorts Isa demanded to see the child. Arian tried to calm him.

"Johanna's making dinner for us. You can share the boy's room while you're here. Believe me, you will see plenty of him! We thought it best to first meet in a place familiar to Nicki rather than this madhouse at the docks."

For Isa, it was love at first sight. He and the boy connected almost instantly. Isa found himself doing things he never thought of doing with his own children. He was having the time of his life. Nicki showed him his shadowboxing techniques and they stumbled around trying to make statutes and vanquish imagined foes. At first Isa didn't understand why the Zantos' were so concerned about him being alone with the boy. Then he cackled to himself.

They have my number. I did come intending to take him one way or another. With the war on in Europe and seeing how well cared for and happy he is here I had forgotten what I meant to do. They are more astute than I had given them credit.

Nicki was two years old when he first met his grandfather. He was fascinated by the man with his white hair and beard. Nicki especially enjoyed the stories of the beautiful young woman who had loved Nicki without ever seeing him. Isa's description of Cassandra's first pony and her adventures with her beautiful mare were the child's favorite of all Isa's tales. Both Arian and Johanna had told him stories many times about the woman who was one of his mothers. She had been his mother until he was born and now she was his Angel Mother who lived in the sky. Nicki thought of her as a cloud floating out of reach above him but didn't understand anything more than that. Cassandra came alive to Nicki in these new stories of the girl's childhood. No longer did he look to the clouds and wonder about this Mother. Isa gave him a picture taken three Summers before. Nicki only had to look on the wall over his bed to see this beautiful woman with a smile that made Nicki break out in a big grin.

Nicki had never understood all of the Angel Mother stories. The sky was so big; he wanted to fly into it and look for this mother. He now understood the part about babies being inside of mothers. That was because of his sister, Ariana, who had certainly made her presence known as she grew inside Mother Johanna. Now once again there was a baby growing inside the tummy of his mother - a tiny little one. Isa predicted this baby would be a boy and hoped he was right as he felt that he was more likely to get his grandson to Greece if Arian had a son of his own.

The first time that Johanna insisted Isa come with her and Nicki to the children's story hour, Isa wasn't sure about such an activity. A woman there asked him to read to the children. He excused himself politely. When Nicki brought him a book and climbed on his knee, Isa began to talk about the pictures. He was not actually reading as his ability to read English was limited, but his monologue caught the attention of children who had heard the written story before.

The pictures were all of animals and Isa was making animal sounds and talking in strange voices.

"This little lamb will grow up to be a big sheep. She will say 'BAA BAA BAA, where are all the other lambs? Are they big too, like me? The men are trying to catch the big ones like me. When they catch them they turn them over and tie their legs together. Then they cut off all their pretty white stuff. They look so funny. They are trying to catch me too. I'd better hide. Where, oh where can I hide?'"

Isa looked up surprised at all the children who gathered round. He turned to one.

JOHANNA

"Where would you hide?"
"In the closet," the child answered.
"I'd hide in the bathroom," another piped in.
"I'd hide under the table," a third said.
Still another spoke. "Why do they want to cut the white stuff off of the sheep?"
"The white stuff is wool," answered Isa. "They take the wool and clean it and then they make it into yarn or cloth. Do you have a wool sweater that you wear in wintertime to keep warm?"
"I do; I do," shouted choruses of children.

Twice Arian took Isa and his family into the heart of Manhattan. Isa saw more people in one hour than in all the time he had lived before. He was amazed by the construction of all the tall buildings. Policeman rode horses through the city streets. The whole panorama drew the eye away from the messes left by the horses. Isa picked up his grandson and carried him on his shoulders. He delighted at the weight of this muscular, healthy boy and carried him with pride.

Once in Manhattan, they stopped to let Nicki watch a parade. There were bands and clowns, tumblers and pretty ladies doing balancing acts on the backs of horses.
"Look, Gramps," Nicki said. "Look at the beautiful women!"
"Yes, this is a circus parade. When you are older I think you will like the circus. Oh look, there are elephants with more girls performing atop. See how they twirl around holding onto the long snouts of the elephants. Cassandra loved the circus from the time she was four years old."
A clown broke ranks with the others and came over to the crowd of people watching. He held the strings of a cluster of balloons; some bright red, some yellow, some two different shades of blue and some a sparkling green.
"Over here," Isa shouted to the clown. "We'll take two

balloons."

The clown separated a green and a yellow balloon from the rest and reached out his hand holding them.

Nicki quickly saw that his grandfather was paying the man and called out.

"Red? Can I have red please?"

A group of about forty ladies holding signs followed the parade.

"Why are they in the circus parade? They just have on clothes like everybody wears." Nicki observed.

"They are suffragettes," Johanna spoke loudly over the din. "They have joined at the end of the parade. They want women to be allowed to vote, like men."

"They are pretty, too," Nicki said. "Look! One is waving to us!"

Almost every day they went to the park with either Zack or Johanna leading the way and with Ariana in Nicki's old stroller. One day they went to the Bronx Zoo and made faces at all the animals. Isa purchased two picture books to share with the children at Pie House; one about monkeys and the other about penguins. They had so much fun at the zoo they went back at least once a week.

In the evenings Isa often joined Arian and Johanna in a poker game, amused that they only played for matches. He found a capable chess partner in Joule and went to the friend's apartment two nights each week. The nights Arian cooked, however, were Isa's favorites.

Isa would be the first to admit he couldn't cook. However, one night Arian was making Baklava when Isa walked in from an early chess night.

"Try it this way if you want the crust thinner." As a very young child Isa had helped his mother make this delicious dessert and some part of his brain had retained every step.

"What else can you cook?" Johanna asked.

"Nothing. Well, maybe if I don't think about it too much I could make a grape pie. I'll get some grapes tomorrow and

JOHANNA

get Nicki to help squash them. I won't promise no mess though, so you may want to veto this idea. Also, I can roast a lamb if you expect a crowd," Isa grinned.

Meanwhile, war broke out full tilt when England joined that Summer, fulfilling the commitment made to France and Russia to stand together if either was attacked. Isa sent several telegrams and received several in return. The fourth week he was in the U.S. he received a packet of letters which included one for Johanna. She opened it to find a note from Piatra advising her to be happy.
You have done the impossible. You have tamed the lion. My father doesn't even sound like himself when he writes about Nicki. He is happy that the boy has such a good home when we're in such an awful sad state of war back here.

Isa stayed three months longer than he had planned. When he left it was without the boy whom he saw to be happy and healthy. However, he would not leave without a signed agreement stating that at the age of thirteen the boy could spend the summer at the vineyard, learning Greek customs and the work of the vineyard. In this way the boy would be able to choose whether he wanted to return to Greece or stay in America as an adult.

Isa had tears in his eyes as he left. How he wanted the boy to choose Greece! However, he could not bring himself to insist and give orders any longer. Not after the tragic results of the demands he had made on his older daughter and the near disaster from the ultimatums he had given his younger daughter.

Arian and Johanna have grasped life by the horns, Isa thought. They now owned four apartment buildings and were decorating for an upscale restaurant on the first floor of their most recent acquisition. Arian no longer worked at the laundry, but was in charge of the construction of the restaurant and doing a great deal of experimental cooking to select specialties for the menu. Johanna helped manage the properties. She kept the accounts in order, billed the tenants and trained the waitresses in the arts of fine dining. Isa would have many stories to tell his family back in Greece.

JOHANNA

CHAPTER TWENTY-SEVEN
PROGRESS
The Bronx, New York
Winter 1914 - 1915

During the months of Isa's visit and the time since then, the project to assist destitute mothers and homeless children flourished.

Renovations to Pie Hall were proceeding rapidly, mostly due to the enthusiasm of Rick and his co-workers. Johanna stopped in every morning to lend a hand and plan with Rita.

Rita was the very soul of Pie Hall. She interviewed applicants, arranged a secret way to send messages to three nearby brothels, took in pregnant women and children of all ages needing care and protection.

"I can't believe you've done such a good job in this apartment," Johanna declared.

"Oh, this is not an apartment," Rita replied as she put the last touches on the mural showing a laughing goat pulling against his rope with a comical man leaning back at the other end. "This room will be for the youngest of infants and will have several beds for them. It includes a play area at one end of the room where potential mothers can meet the children. The babies can stay here until they are eighteen months old then we can move them into the larger nursery we finished two months ago.

"Of course, little Susan may have to stay here longer as her development is slow. June, our newest live-in adult, has just started working with her to shake a rattle, clap her hands and other simple tasks. We hope this will help."

Johanna hugged Rita. "You are the light that brightens

this place. You give it strength and personality. Just about everyone who comes to look at the children takes one, and some take two. I had two more letters this morning requesting visits. So far ten babies have been placed and are there are fourteen living here with or without mothers."

"Isn't it about time we decided on the business up front," Rita proposed as she picked up a wiggling ten month old needing a diaper change.

"It seems to be creating itself - a children's book store with scheduled events like reading aloud to varying age groups," Johanna proposed as she moved the soiled diaper to the laundry hamper. "Maybe we could add a toy store and a newborn or maybe 'under two' gift shop. The little crocheted hat and sweaters you just finished are great and will bring in customers - some who will possibly become interested in a baby.

Rita smiled at Johanna as she spoke, "I've started a list of needs we have to address before actually hanging out a shingle. Do you think we could go over it together some evening after the babies are asleep. There are so many interruptions here.

"I hate to tell you but the older children are outnumbering our spaces," Rita continued. "They are sleeping on the floor in the halls. Will you ask your husband if we can have more of the downstairs for more dormitories? Or maybe a place on a higher level? Since we started helping them, more and more homeless boys have shown up at our door."

"Yes, of course I will, but I have to do it soon. All the men are riled up over the recent news of the war in Europe. They are meeting soon to discuss action. I am afraid it's action involving actual confrontation."

"Maybe that explains why Arian and Zack were here with another boy I don't know. They gathered all the boys over twelve and talked to them. I couldn't hear without eavesdropping."

JOHANNA

CHAPTER TWENTY-EIGHT
DARK CLOUDS
1915

The flight of time is measured for many by minutes and hours - by days and weeks. For some it is measured by tears and for others by laughter. The time of 'The Great War' was at hand. Within this war the seeds were sown for even greater bloodshed and destruction. Violence begets violence; sorrow begets sorrow and joy begets joy.

Arian was involved in a dark discussion. He was a warrior at heart and news of the war disturbed him greatly. Joule arranged a meeting of several leaders of the groups which still strongly supported Albania, their native country.

"We have earned our independence only to have it threatened again," Joule began. "Our first decision must be which side to take. There are dangers either way."

"Yes," said Arian. "I have heard the Austrians have offered Greece half of Albania if they will give up enough of Greece to bribe Belgium to join them. In addition, Austria is aligned with our old enemy, the Turks."

"My sources say the same." Joule stated. "I for one must align with Britain. They are sworn to protect the neutrality of Greece, where my family is now."

"I stand with Joule," came a chorus around the table. One raised his mug and the men shouted and laughed as they drank to war. Like Arian, their passionate natures led them to embrace conflict.

Arian quieted the group by raising his hand.

"What we need are runners; men who can move quickly

and quietly by horseback, foot or mule. We need to inform the Allies of plans of the Austrians and the Bulgars aligned with them. All who volunteer stay after for assignments. For others I will talk come morning. Who will join me. I need someone to train recruits who've never ridden a horse! It will be difficult leaving. The women and older men will need to deal with whatever comes up, but it can't be helped. I'm sure they will rise to the challenge."

The mountains of Albania are fearsome to those who do not know the paths. Arian had spent his childhood living in the mountains. His family found shelter and safety in the treacherous terrain. The family had dedicated their lives to resisting the forces who occupied their country. Their skill in navigating the mountain paths aided them in this endeavor. Arian hated leaving his family here in the Bronx, but he could not avoid the call of his native land.
"Joule, you will be in charge of recruits. We will not join any formal army, but must be prepared for guerilla duty coordinated by our own people. Send any man you can't trust to join a Canadian regiment. Collect only the most able and most trustworthy. I'll go at once to Albania or to Northern Greece if I can't get through to the homeland. Our friends will try to hide some boats in a deserted part of the Ionian Sea - this side. We may have fighters or civilians who need to escape."
"I'd prefer to go with you, you know that!" Joule sighed. "But I understand what I need to do first. I'll start with a trip to Detroit to recruit the healthiest and most loyal.
"Your presence in the homeland may be necessary soon. Refugees are already gathering in Serbia and will need guides to escape through the mountains. I have several young scouts. I will teach them the main paths from Serbia to the sea, over the mountains. There will come a day when many must take that path. We will be ready for the refugees and the enemy."

JOHANNA

CHAPTER TWENTY-NINE
UPHEAVAL

Arian had discussed with Johanna the need he felt to go back to Albania to assist his countrymen in this time of great need. When told more specifics and the plan to go right away, Johanna tried to hide her disappointment, but not her pride.

Not only would she miss Arian, but there was so much to be done on the home front. Johanna questioned her ability to handle things alone. She managed to get through breakfast with a smile. There would be no lingering over coffee today.

Shortly after Arian kissed Johanna and left to finalize travel arrangements, a boy arrived with a telegram. A few weeks before, Johanna received a letter from an assistant of her father's advising her that Franklin was sending Sybil to their country home for the duration of the war and to send all mail there. Today the cryptic telegraph simply read: "Sybil sick with fright. Bringing her to you." As simple as the telegraph was it foreboded misery. If her mother was sick she certainly did not need to be coming here.

That evening Arian called. He would be a little later than their usual dinner, but he would be home to pack, eat and sleep. By dawn he would be on his way to Europe.

"Should I even mention the telegram?" Johanna worried silently.

With Ariana only a few months old, Nikki feeling his three-year old oats, the new baby growing inside of her, and Arian leaving and in possible danger, Johanna felt overwhelmed. Her mother was always hard to deal with, even in best of times.

"At least I can count on Zack for help," she sighed. "I wonder what Mother will think of tea served in stoneware mugs and my efforts to help orphans."

Ariana was just awaking from her nap when Zack came in, bringing Nicki with him.

"The women are closing the bookstore early today so they can say good-bye to a contingent of people heading for Canada. It seems for some of them the chance to make good money from lonely soldiers won out over their desire for a new profession."

"How many are going, do you know?"

"About half. I've sent word to my brother. Now is his time to leave if ever he will have one. He is coming to live in my place while I am gone and to help you. I know he is young but he can run errands and he learns quickly."

"You are leaving? Then are you going to join the Canadian Armed Forces? Or someone else's?" Johanna tried to keep the disappointment out of her voice.

"No. I'm going with Arian. I always wanted to ride a horse. Besides they will draft me if I am here when we Americans join the War and I don't think that will be long."

"I am going to miss both of you. Can I meet your brother tonight - better still, within the hour?"

"I sent him taxi fare and this address. I'll go and pack quickly. Why don't you come with me Nicki? It will be fun helping me pack."

"Can I go Mommy? Can I?" Nicki asked excitedly.

Johanna smiled and gave Nicki a kiss as well as her permission.

Arian arrived home before Zack and his brother, Noah.

"Maybe they are giving us some time alone," Johanna hoped.

"If only we knew just when they would pop right in," Arian put his arms around Johanna. "Are both children

JOHANNA

asleep?"

"Only Ariana. Zack took Nicki to help him pack."

"Now I think you're right about time alone," Arian mused.

Arian's kisses surrounded her neck, arousing her. Their kisses started slowly, then deepened in both urgency and passion. As they headed toward the bedroom the phone rang.

"Oh, let it be someone else's ring on this party line."

Counting out the rings they nodded at one another and Johanna picked up the phone. Her voice was deeper than usual because of the kisses Arian continued to place on the back of her neck.

"Is this Mrs. Johanna Zantos? I hope I don't have the wrong number. I'm Betty Skendar, her new tenant in building 12, apartment 2 and it is urgent that I reach her."

"Yes, I am Johanna. What is wrong?"

"There is a very dirty little boy here. He got out of a taxi with an old duffle bag and a huge burlap bag that looks to weigh a ton. He thought this was your address and let the cab go, though he has a slip of paper with your address written clearly. I don't know how he can manage to get the three blocks to you with this stuff and I'm afraid to let him in my house."

"That must be Noah. Do you remember when you picked up your keys last Monday you admired the carving on my desk."

"Oh, yes it is the most lovely carving of an eagle that I have ever seen - of any bird in flight, actually."

"Well, the dirty little boy you see with the bags is the carver. He is coming to stay with us while his brother is away. I can't explain the dirt right now. Could you keep the bags for now and give him walking directions? The bags are most likely more carvings or the materials needed to make more. His brother would come and pick him up, but he is not here right now."

"So long as you can vouch for him, I'll try to get another cab and you can reimburse me later."

"If you are willing to let him stay there as soon as Zack gets here I will send him for Noah. You remember Zack - he is the young man who repainted your bedroom just before you moved in. I'm glad you called. Thank you so much for helping. Goodbye."

Johanna hung up the phone and turned to Arian.

"Now, back to the business at hand," Arian whispered, checking the lock on the outer door. Lifting Johanna in his arms, he carried her into their bedroom, carefully closing the door.

"We'll make this a quick one, and plan for longer when the brothers are out of here and Nicki is sleeping."

"Lie back then and let me take the initiative," Johanna meowed, baring her breasts and leaning toward Arian as she sat astride him.

The knock on the door came before Arian could get out of his shower. Betty Skendar arrived with Noah and a cabdriver dragging the heavy bags. The cabbie was another immigrant from Albania and a great fan of Arian. He refused to take the fare, drawing Arian to the far side of the room from the women and boy.

"I would like to shake your hand. I've admired your courage when you were in Albania before. I hear you are going back," he whispered.

Arian nodded toward the strange woman - a woman he had never seen before.

"It's alright," the cabbie said. "She is my cousin. Her husband, Dan, well actually Dardan, but we just call him Dan, is leaving early tomorrow. I'd go too but they tell me I'm too old. They did sign me on for local transport."

"They weren't to take men with babies on the way. She must be about six months," Arian said.

"Betty and Dan talked it over. They decided not to

JOHANNA

mention it."

"She's a little ahead of Johanna. We'll need to be back before the births," Arian sighed hoping that they would make it in time.

Zack arrived before the cabbie left. Arian introduced them.

"Zack, this is Al Arber. He has just agreed to keep an eye on the ladies holding down the homestead. He belongs to the taxi outside."

Johanna and Betty had tea and corned beef ready with thick slices of cheese and fresh baked bread. Noah won the prize for the biggest appetite eating as much as any three of the others could eat in the same time period.

After Noah promised Johanna to arrive back by ten the next morning, he left with Zack for Zack's apartment. Al gave Betty a ride home and Arian had some alone time with Nicki while a sleepy Ariana accompanied her mother into the bathtub, having been awakened by all the people.

It was almost midnight before Arian and Johanna were alone again.

"Now, I'm in charge," Arian declared. In his arms Johanna quickly became aroused. What game would he want to play tonight?

Arian rubbed her shoulders.

"You are tense, tonight. We will have to do something about that. Just close your eyes and pretend we are sitting in a tree. The large branch we are perched on is ample for us to lie back. But if I roll to one side I have to flip you over and take you with me - oh, better to balance you on my legs so I can keep you safely in the tree.

As he spoke Arian effortlessly lifted Johanna, first flipping her over and caressing her lower back and lower.

Next he bent his knees and gave her a bouncing ride atop his calves. Johanna laughed in delight.

"Oh, look. I found fruit in this tree. Is it a grapevine

filled with juicy fruit - or perhaps - yes I think I found a peach. I'd better taste it to be sure."

"I found a banana but it must be too green to eat - it is really hard," Johanna giggled.

JOHANNA

CHAPTER THIRTY
KNOWS NO BOUNDARIES

Johanna stirred as she heard Arian moving quietly around the room gathering his things. It was just before dawn with only a little light coming through the window. She forced herself to wake up realizing what was happening.

"Good morning," Johanna said as her bare feet touched the cold floor. She reached for the bedside lamp and turned it on. "This will help you find things," she said. "Should I go and make coffee?"

"I was hesitant to wake you," Arian said. "But before I left I was going to kiss you goodbye. If I thought there was time for coffee I'd put better use to the minutes." He took Johanna in his arms. "Always remember the joys we have shared here. I will find strength in your memory. I will return as soon as possible, hopefully before the new baby comes. Once I have trained enough people as guides as necessary I will try my best return to you. Meanwhile I will live on our memories which are more vital to me than food. Communications may be difficult but I will write and post when I can."

Johanna nodded.

"I wish I had an address to write to you.

"Write anyway. Send letters to Nicki's grandfather with the ones to me sealed inside. I'll try to get messages from there since it is close to the border. If something urgent comes up send him a wire. They use carrier pigeons at his vineyard. I think Erjon already has something arranged with Piatra or so I've heard."

Thank you for that. It'll mean so much to be in contact."

Johanna hugged Arian. Neither wanted to break the embrace and when they did it was almost at the same instant.

"I won't say goodbye," Johanna said. "I will say bon voyage."

As Johanna and Nicki were finishing breakfast they heard a loud knock on the door.

"That must be Noah. He is here early," Johanna yawned, still sleepy after the hectic dawn goodbyes to loved ones and the hellos to the new people now sharing their lives.

"Noah is funny. He makes toy talk," Nicki said, smiling.

Johanna looked carefully at the boy. Not even to his third birthday he was strong, tall and handsome. Was it all the shadow boxing and gymnastics Zack had taught him or had his size come from his Grandfather, Isa? Certainly, he did look somewhat like Isa if a toddler can look like a man well along in years. Old, maybe, but Isa was strong, too, and if Niccolò was anything like his brother the strength came from blood ties on both sides.

"Come in, Noah. The door isn't locked." Johanna rose with the intent of getting a mug for tea for Noah.

"My daughter," a man's voice broke the silence. "Maturity becomes you." Franklin Bennett embraced his daughter carefully, hands placed on either shoulder but without any other body contact. He had a catch in his voice - the most emotion Johanna remembered observing from him ever.

"I - I'll just go for the luggage and to pay the driver. Go on in, Sybil, you're blocking the door."

Johanna's mother looked twenty years older than when they were last together. She held herself rigid until Johanna walked toward her.

"Wait," muttered Sybil, holding her hand up with palm open and flat, bidding her daughter to stop. As soon as the door closed Sybil advanced.

"You fool. You detestable, despicable excuse for a daughter."

JOHANNA

Her arm swung and her flat hand struck Johanna's left cheek. Then the back of Sybil's hand followed with a slap to the right. Johanna staggered and grabbed a chair behind her for support. Two more slaps and she was on her knees.

"You are no better than a common whore. You could have been a Duchess. Think of the life we could have had you selfish bitch. What happened to your Italian stud? Now what? What rogue, nobody are you living with and what kind of offspring will that bastard be. You have no concern for your mother and her ruined insides delivering you into this world. I should have smothered you the day you were born! You ungrateful bitch."

Taken by surprise and trying to protect her belly from the unwanted blows, Johanna heard Ariana screaming. Johanna was reaching for the foot that was about to land directly on her middle.

Suddenly, there was a loud crash as Nicki tackled the intruder in a flying leap, having first attached his football helmet - a gift from Zack.

As Sybil fell she hit her head on the inside of the door just as Franklin returned and was pushing it open from outside the room. Sybil was out cold.

Nicki cheered with his hands over his head like he and Zack did when ball players scored touchdowns or got a ball in the high up baskets.

Ariana screamed.

Franklin fainted.

Only then did Noah arrive and surveyed the scene, possibly with an inclination to run.

Nicki broke the silence.

"Mean woman hurt Earth Mommy," he told Noah. "I tackled her like they do in football when sometimes Zack takes me to see. Will you take me too?"

"Right now we had better see about Johanna."

"Earth Mommy is strong," Nicki went to Johanna. "Maybe not so strong. She has blood on her face."

Franklin was coming around. Beneath Ariana's screams

he heard the word blood.

"What on earth happened here?" he asked.

"You brought a bad woman. She hurt my Mommy. I tackled her and made her stop," Nicki said bravely as the man stared at him.

"What did you hit her with? Did you see what happened?" Franklin turned toward Noah.

"When I got here the door was open and all you grownups were laying on the floor. I am going to get Ariana and take her and Nicki to be with Mrs. Skendar. I'll tell her to call an ambulance – or do you need a cop? Is she dead?"

Johanna crawled over to her mother.

"She has a pulse beat. She hit the door with the back of her head just as you were opening it, Father. I don't think we should move her until someone else comes. Noah would you call Al Arber. The number is on the notepad under the phone."

"I - I can't read; I'm sorry. They wouldn't let us learn."

Franklin was wide-eyed at that. He had heard America was uncivilized, but this...

"I'll try," he offered.

"You don't need to read." Nicki promptly went to the phone, picked up the receiver and said, "We have bloody people here and one won't wake up. Please let us use the phone now."

Franklin raised his eyebrows.

"They have more requests than lines," Johanna explained. "We have a four-party and three different families share one of them. Tell them our names, Nicki. Ask them to get help to us."

JOHANNA

CHAPTER THIRTY-ONE
BEING THERE

"Let's not move her until a doctor or nurse arrives," Sally, one of the party-line neighbors advised. The call for help had brought four assorted people, all talking or eavesdropping when Nicki picked up the phone.

Franklin Bennett recovered enough to agree before he excused himself and went into the bathroom.

Nicki came and lay beside Johanna, whispering in her ear, "Stay here with you or see Ariana."

"Oh would you please go to Ariana. Tell her not to be afraid. If you can, help her out of her crib or get one of these people to help you." With a kiss to the forehead she sent him to her daughter.

Johanna got up off the floor with help, gratefully accepting a chair from a young man with a limp. She had not seen him before but guessed he must be 'ring four.'

"I'm Sam Nagel, unfortunate way to meet," he noted. "You took some heavy blows to your face. Are you hurt anywhere else."

"Right now it seems like everywhere. How is Mother?"

"The woman on the floor is your mother? Who hit you - the man?"

"No. Maybe you could see if he is ok. I think he fainted. I've never seen Mother so angry before. I am reeling more from her words than her blows."

"Sally is looking after her. She nursed her sick father for years. I'll check on your father and see if someone has called medical help. You promise not to get up without someone to help."

"Yes, of course. Do you know what happened to Noah?"

"If he was a young kid, he was running out the door when I came in, yelling something about Missus someone."

Johanna tried to smile but it hurt too much. "He is going for help from the only person he has met here. I hope Betty can come. She is good with the children."

Shortly, Sam returned with Franklin.

"We are going to carry you to bed - to lie down where it's quieter. The children want to lie beside you. I told them maybe if they could be still. Mrs. Wheaton has the little one all dry and clean."

"I'm surprised Ariana let a stranger help her."

"I was watching from the door," Franklin admitted, greatly surprising his daughter. "My little granddaughter has a lot of spunk. She said, 'Stranger's don't touch me,' clear as a bell. Your little boy told her 'This is Molly, ring one, she sings on phone.'

"Ariana looked at this woman with wide eyes, getting wider as the woman started singing 'Mary Had a Little Lamb' to her."

By the time Noah arrived with Betty, Molly Wheaton had the children settled in bed with Johanna and was joining her 'talking' friend, making breakfast. Sally was monitoring Sybil's pulse count. She had covered the woman with two blankets, but refused to move her to even put a pillow under her head. Sam had taken Franklin into the children's bedroom to lie down.

Franklin was exhausted from the trip from England. His anxiety had increased daily as his wife's condition deteriorated. He staggered when he tried to walk. He was no sooner in a prone position than his snores began.

Sam chose the rocking chair and nodded off also. He liked all this excitement, much better than just listening in. Even with his limp, maybe he should get out more.

JOHANNA

CHAPTER THIRTY-TWO
WATCH OUT ABOVE YOU
Near a Battlefield in Albania

Arian's group of twelve guerillas practiced stealth and quickness for two weeks before coming to Albania. Their mission was to report to the regular armies. Specifically, report to Canadian troops. They were to watch for the movement of enemy battalions and to stall them if possible, doing so stealthily. Also, they were to send the Red Cross a runner if they could find a route for refugees to travel through the mountains safely.

Arian heard the arrow whiz by him as he hovered near the top of a huge oak tree.

"Someone signaling," he muttered under his breath. If the arrow had been aimed at a straight angle, it might have wounded him, but it had been shot straight up in the sky.

It was only minutes when he heard Zack's bird call. Someone else was nearby and even the sounds of birds could mean danger.

From Arian's left he heard another tweet - exactly the one chosen for one of the Albanian home contingent to connect with those from the Bronx. Arian breathed a sign of relief and gave the third whistle.

Soon the stranger and Zack had swung into Arian's leafy roost, helped by the wild grape vines the thickness of a man's arm.

"Are you from the Monk?" Arian asked, looking closely at the newcomer.

"No questions. Follow me," the newcomer replied.

Zack was having none of this.

"How do we know you will not lead us into ambush?"

"It's all right, Zack," Arian interrupted. "I believe I know this young man. If he looks closely at my face he will know me too, as I look like my brother."

"My orders are 'Silence'. Scouts are everywhere. I've had to kill two on the way here." Erjon scampered to an upper branch from which he could reach the grapevine. Pushing off with both feet against the tree he swung to the next and sent the vine sailing back for Arian and Zack.

The next sound they heard was a man's heavy snore. As the training had emphasized, the third man back descended lower in the tree, attempting to identify the source of the sound.

It was critical to either get by the guard undetected or to kill him quietly before he could cry out for help. Zack had to make the decision as he was the point man looking at the enemy.

First question - is he the enemy? As silently as death Zack reached the lowest branch. The man wore a civilian outfit and carried a gunny sack with some mushrooms showing at the opening and a civilian knife.

OOPS.

This is a setup, Zack realized. The man wore Army issued boots and it wasn't the season for gathering mushrooms. Even the man's snore wasn't rhythmic. Zack made his decision: KILL!

JOHANNA

CHAPTER THIRTY-THREE
ONE STEP BEHIND
The Bronx, New York

Franklin put down the phone. "I don't know if it's good news or bad news."

Franklin and Johanna had waited anxiously for over a week to hear more about Sybil's condition.

"That was a person from the hospital. They're not willing to keep Sybil any longer. She is not in a coma. Her vital signs are good and she can feed herself at least partially, However, she does not respond to voice directions, or speak at all. They're sending her to Manhattan State Asylum for a psychiatric evaluation. She will be admitted there this afternoon. They want to keep her for a minimum of six months for evaluation. Her psychiatrist will be a physician named Michael Freeman. They have given us his phone number and suggest we make an appointment for further questions."

"Poor Mother," Johanna sighed. "I should've been in touch more often and much sooner. I never imagined Mother in such a state as this...."

"She has been going downhill for months. It is not your fault: it is the war. Your mother was made for happy times, for parties, dances and afternoon teas. That is what I always tried to give her, especially when I didn't have to accompany her. I was made for banking hours which, unknown to many, means very long hours at work. She was happiest when Elizabeth was there visiting, her outgoing ways resulting in many extra invitations. Now she never sees Elizabeth and fears she never will again with Elizabeth in India. Losing

Elizabeth and you at the same time was too much for her. You were her admission ticket to what she considered her life."

"Well, no use regretting what is past. We can only do something about the present and future," Johanna remarked. "Let's make this appointment with Dr. Michael Freeman and visit her often. How long can you stay in America?"

"Not much longer I'm afraid. I was supposed to be back three days ago. I have extended it for another week but I can't stay much longer. With this war I'm afraid it is more important that I be in London than ever before."

The waiting room was decorated in pale greens and a light beige. Several attractively framed pictures hung on the wall; some pencil sketches and some watercolors. Johanna walked around examining the pictures as she waited. One especially caught her eye as it looked so familiar. It showed an old steamship with passengers walking up the ramp, carrying heavy burdens. The varied and bulky luggage gave proof to the impression that these were emigrants headed for a new life in a new place. Just a simple pencil sketch, still it held a great deal of detail. On one area of the ship there were printed letters: definitely the beginning letter was an 'M.' Johanna's memory rushed back in time. She was looking at a real scene very similar to this from a pier in Sicily. Goose bumps popped out all over her arms.

Just as she turned she heard her name called. The psychiatrist himself greeted them and ushered them into his office. Dr. Freeman was a well-dressed, healthily built man in his late 30s. He greeted them warmly. Instead of sitting behind his desk he beckoned them to three comfortable chairs in front of the double window of the corner office.

"We're just beginning our examination," the psychiatrist started. "From the information we have collected from the acute hospital here in New York and the persons who were treating Mrs. Bennett in London, our initial diagnosis is

JOHANNA

catatonic schizophrenia. This form of schizophrenia tends to occur in middle-age and has a higher percentage of recoveries than other types. This particular illness is manifested in two extreme ways. Sometimes the patient is unresponsive to most other people as if in a stupor. Other times the patient is excitable, unpredictable, and agitated. One of these extremes can persist for many days – even months or they can vacillate sometimes even within the same hour. We need a careful observation over a period of several months to know if this is truly Mrs. Bennett's problem or if she has an organic condition due to brain injury connected to her fall. The fact that she was having symptoms before though, before the fall that is, make us think that her condition started much earlier and explains her aggressive attack on her daughter."

"Can we visit her today? I have extended my stay here in New York for about as long as I can. I have to leave in a week and I would like to take her back to London with me for treatment there."

"I would strongly advise you not to have her travel anytime in the near future. The various stimuli on board a steamer could cause a severe reaction that might endanger her or someone else. As for visiting her today I will allow it for you, but not for Mrs. Zantos. It seems like you are part of her delusion, Mrs. Zantos, and her reaction to you might lead to another disturbance. I would like to see her able to express herself in words and resolve some of her anger towards you before you visit. Or at least I would like to wait until she can respond knowingly to the idea of a visit with you and how she feels about the same. Just one moment and I'll have an escort to take you down to the visiting area, Mr. Bennett."

Dr. Freeman was back shortly.

"It seems we are somewhat short of staff today for escort purposes. One of our people just had an emergency at home. I will walk down with you and show you the library near the visitor's room, Mrs. Zantos. I think you will find something of interest there while your father and mother visit."

Franklin Bennett was ushered into a pleasant visiting room to await Sybil. Dr. Freeman took Johanna's arm and walked further with her.

"I noticed you looked upset as I called you into the office, as if you just had a major shock."

"You're very observant, Dr. Freeman. One of your pictures in the waiting room reminded me of the ship I came here on – the Matilda. It looks so like the Matilda, which brings back old memories, some quite sad."

"Yes, I thought you'd seen the picture - quite impressive isn't it. There are more in the library by the same patient. It is not often that someone looks at the picture twice in the waiting room. However when they come to the library, all seem to be impressed."

If Dr. Freeman had not been standing next to her, Johanna would've fallen. There were six pictures altogether but the one that mattered most was the one that Johanna saw first. Here she was, Johanna, in her hat and scarf standing on the upper deck of the Matilda. It was Johanna's face, Johanna's hat, Johanna's scarf wrapped around her shoulders, with one end blowing in the wind like her hair that had loosened from it's knot.

In the lower left of the picture stood a beautiful girl dressed in a cloak that was loose, flying open, propelled by the strong winds. She was reaching up for an orange that was coming toward her through the air.

"I was utterly amazed when I saw your face. The resemblance is uncanny. You threw the orange to our Jane, then? Jane doesn't know her real name. When I saw you looking at the boat and then saw your face more clearly in the office I hoped you would be able to tell us something more about the girl."

"Cassandra. Cassandra is her name. They told me she had died in child birth. I can't believe she drew these. May I sit down? I don't think I can stand."

JOHANNA

"Of course, let me help you." Dr. Freeman assisted Johanna to a comfortable chair then continued. "She had been very ill according to the initial records they kept at the infirmary on Ellis Island. An old woman was with her the first day she was taken to the infirmary. The woman would not leave her side so we thought they were related. When the older woman's son came to claim her, she tried to convince him to take the girl. He turned to us and explained in English. I've been over it so many times I remember almost verbatim what is written in the record.

"'*What she wants is impossible. She is such a beautiful girl. My wife is the jealous type. She would never stand for such a beautiful girl to move in with us. There is absolutely no way. Not even for a few days. Besides, I did not bring enough money to show I can support my mother and another woman.*'

"The older woman began talking again in the language the staff did not know. She gave a packet of powders to a nearby employee and pantomimed instructions that she put a spoonful in the girl's tea three times a day for one more week. The son, again, interpreted for her.

"'*She gathers medicinal herbs and they always seem to help people. My mother had quite a reputation in the villages where we lived.*'

"The younger woman stepped forward and hugged the older. The son became impatient. The report goes on to say that someone examined the powders and found it to be a mint tea. The staff were drinking it though the week. No one would admit giving it to the patient, which of course would not be an acceptable practice.

"Do you know Cassandra's full name? The patient we called Jane?"

"No - yes - yes I do." Johanna was weeping silently, overcome with emotion. "A ship's seaman brought the little baby newly born. He told me that his mother didn't make it; I thought him to mean she had died in childbirth. I took the child to wet nurse. Maybe he said the baby wouldn't make it unless I nursed him. I was very confused. My own baby and my husband had been taken from me with no ceremony to be buried at sea. When the seaman brought me the baby boy at first I thought my daughter had revived. I was very cold, especially my feet. Looking down at them I saw that I had no shoes. I don't remember leaving my cabin, yet I was found climbing down to the lower deck, wanting to get to the water."

"Did the seaman give you a name for the baby or his mother?" Dr. Freeman asked.

"No. I discovered letters in the cloak which the baby was wrapped in when brought to me. I am sure it was her's as I had seen her wear it when we were both outside on pleasant days. She was the only one on board who was anywhere close to term, except me and my daughter wasn't due for at least two months. Her son brought me back to life. I can't wait to have him meet her."

Suddenly the psychiatrist's face turned ashen.

"She has a living son, then. Oh my God, what have we done? We judged that to be a delusion. Her insistence that her son was healthy and robust and alive we thought was unreal, delusional. That was the basis for an initial diagnosis. We must find her."

"What do you mean, find her. Isn't she here with all her drawings? I must see her."

"She has been gone more than a year. I don't know where she is but I'll find her. I must." Freeman was obviously in great anguish.

Johanna spoke quietly at first.

"You were more than Cassandra's doctor- I can tell by your expression. Don't deny it. It will make matters worse."

"It is not what you're thinking. I never touched her. Physically I was able to maintain my professional persona. How I wanted the relationship to be different is what you are seeing. From the beginning on Ellis Island I fell deeply in love. I took charge of her care and moved her here where I work.

JOHANNA

"I thought it was what was best for her. She was definitely depressed and deeply so. Also, she must have been in some kind of accident or been beaten in the head. She had amnesia and didn't remember anything before arriving at the Island's infirmary. Well, nothing except a male child which she insisted she kept and fed for at least one night. It is very unusual in my experience to remember one thing and not anything else. I added delusional to her diagnosis on this basis."

"It sounds like the diagnosis was correct considering the varied memories," Johanna conceded.

"You can't understand. I was called away due to a family crisis and was gone for five weeks. My colleagues took charge and ordered electric shock therapy - many treatments. When I returned all the progress she and I had made was wiped out. She was happy as a lark and asked for her horse, but everything else in her life was forgotten. It took two years to get her back to the point we had been."

"So she got better before she left? She isn't a vegetable in some nursing facility?" Johanna asked.

"No, not her. She is the most unflappable, determined woman I ever met in my life. Her one reason to live is to find her family - the baby and his father. All other men are non-existent to her. Several men - from nurses to patients - have given it their best effort, but she doesn't even seem to understand what they desire."

"So you just let her go?"

"No. She made friends with a volunteer who led a needlework class. Then the orders came through that women stable enough could help the war effort by moving to the areas where factories needed workers. They could care for school aged children if they could not work directly in a factory. She was a better seamstress than anyone here. The volunteer joined our program for patients ready to leave. It was designed to give patients families to live with when leaving here. Jane - ah - Cassandra was there for about six weeks. Then she left suddenly.

"The volunteer's daughter had turned fourteen and was invited to an overnight party. The volunteer was transporting her daughter when Cassandra disappeared. She reported that people had often given Cassandra tips when they dropped by to pick up embroidered baby clothes or collars. She must have called a taxi to get to the train or bus. At any rate she left no information as to her whereabouts. I'm going to start by going through my old records to look for possible ties."

The baby inside Johanna began to wiggle and kick vigorously. It was the baby's first movements Johanna had felt and she smiled delightedly.

"When Mother attacked me I was worried that the consequences could be dire," Johanna said at the Doctor's puzzled expression. "Now the baby is making its presence known.

"The varied emotions that I am feeling now regarding Cassandra are heart-stirring, as in stirred with an egg beater. I feel a powerful joy and overwhelming relief. She is well and functioning. She will be reunited with little Nicki. I have felt it many times in my heart. However, most likely we'll never find Cassandra. Somehow, someway, Cassandra will find us!"

The End

Made in the USA
Charleston, SC
20 October 2014